HEAR YOUR BRAIN
WHISPER

HOW TO UNLOCK YOUR MIND'S POTENTIAL

OTAKARA KLETTKE

ISBN: 978-0-9979070-6-3

Copyright © 2020 Otakara Klettke

All rights reserved. No part of this publication may be reproduced, distributed, or transmitted in any form or by any means, including photocopying, recording, or other electronic or mechanical methods, without the prior written permission of the publisher, except in the case of brief quotations embodied in reviews and certain other noncommercial uses permitted by copyright law.

Disclaimer

The information in this book is based on author's own experience and research.

It is the reader's own responsibility to consult a physician or therapist before using information provided in this book. One's health symptoms may require proper diagnosis or professional medical attention.

DEDICATION

To my Mom

Links to free gifts

An exercise that promotes an increase in positive neurotransmitters
https://otakaraklettke.com/exercise

30-Day Sleep Challenge to create a routine that enables deep sleep
https://otakaraklettke.com/sleep

Meditation that takes you on a healing journey inside your body
https://otakaraklettke.com/meditation

Table of Contents

Introduction		1
Chapter 1:	Every Brain is Unique	7
Chapter 2:	Basic Structure, Function, and Communication	13
Chapter 3:	How Is a Thought Born?	23
Chapter 4:	Can the Body Heal the Brain?	27
Chapter 5:	Improving Your Brain	33
Chapter 6:	Accessing the Subconscious Mind	47
Chapter 7:	Subliminal Perception	53
Chapter 8:	Intelligence	59
Chapter 9:	What Can We Learn from Psychopaths?	65
Chapter 10:	Brain's Drugs and Functions	73
Chapter 11:	This Is Your Brain on Drugs	83
Chapter 12:	Memory	93
Chapter 13:	Sleep	105
Chapter 14:	Sex	117
Chapter 15:	Flow	123
Chapter 16:	Brain's Blues	129
Chapter 17:	Exercise	139
Chapter 18:	Meditation	145
Chapter 19:	Goodbye	151
About the Author		153

Introduction

"I'm always doing something. I never shut my brain off. I always have something going on."

Angelina Jolie

Would you want your loved ones to pull the plug if you were brain-dead?

It is a scary question to ponder. The truth is, if someone is brain-dead, he or she is pronounced dead by the doctors. The body is not kept alive unless the person was registered as a donor and, in that case, the body is only kept alive until the organs can be harvested.

Pardon me for giving you a trick question. The decision to pull the plug comes in when someone ends up in a vegetative state, wherein their brain is not fully dead. There is always some brain activity and the person in that state drifts in and out of consciousness often without anyone in their surroundings realizing.

When I posted this question on Facebook, most people responded with, "I'd want the plug pulled." It shows how much we treasure this fatty gray wrinkly blob inside our heads. In case you're wondering, my relationship with this question is somewhat complicated.

When my mom was in her late teens, she had a non-cancerous tumor in her brain. She collapsed into a coma and was transported to the hospital. My mom told me that when they brought her to the hospital, she regained consciousness for a moment but was unable to let anyone know. She heard the doctor say, "Why are you bringing a living corpse in here?"

She was the second person in the former Czechoslovakia to have brain surgery. This was in the late 1950s. The surgery was successful, but it took a year out of my mom's young and promising life. She spent weeks in a coma and forgot the basics — how to walk, how to talk — and had to learn these things all over again. Thankfully, learning was my mom's forte. After her recovery, she got a Ph.D. in botany and another one in teaching a decade later. Her brain was phenomenal despite everything she had been through.

The truth is that everything involving the brain is uncertain. It is, without a doubt, the most fascinating organ we have. While the rest of the body can technically survive without a functioning brain with the help of modern medicine, it is the only organ most people do not want to live without. In case it is barely functioning, the brain is one organ for which doctors are willing to let the body die.

At certain times, when the brain is faced with challenges such as malfunction, disease, injury, over or underproduction of neurotransmitters etc., it changes the person who carries it. It does not alter the soul of the individual, but to that person's family it may seem like it does. Attention deficit disorder, depression, anxiety, dementia, stroke, cancer, and many other conditions can leave a person utterly changed.

Everything that makes you feel emotions is the result of the chemicals that your body or brain produces. Imagine, for instance, that your brain has a bar. It makes cocktails that it consumes or sends out to the rest of the body. In return, the body sends food and other cocktails to the brain. The goal of this book is to not only introduce you to the bartender in your brain bar, but to help them become a better one.

On the other hand, pharmaceutical pills are designed to mess with these chemicals. I aim to show you what you can do to let your body create its own medicine, as well as help you understand the basics regarding those bodily substances.

Please note that quitting pharmaceutical medication that

affects the brain is extremely dangerous! If you are taking any, do not choose to stop without consulting a doctor.

Brain medication is not like most other medication. Extreme caution must be exercised. Do not use this book as a reason to quit any kind of psychiatric pills. That step must be taken only under the supervision of a professional. Now that we have got that out of the way, we can and will work together to master your brain.

How you feel is an inside job. I am sure you have already heard that somewhere. I mean it in the exact sense. It is an inside job because how you feel is dependent on your brain. It all depends on the cocktail party happening inside your brain. When you understand how brain chemicals affect you, you will be able to put yourself in the state of mind —or better said, state of your brain — that allows you to be your best self.

Imagine what you can achieve when your brain is tuned up! Not only would you be capable of addressing issues that an untuned brain is causing, but you could also achieve the highest potential that is within you. It is important to become balanced and supported by beneficial neurotransmitters, such as oxytocin and dopamine. The feelings caused by the healthy release of these hormones will enable you to move towards your goals with excitement and enthusiasm. It is similar to the feeling of being in love. When infatuated, everything is much easier to achieve. But, unless you are immune to heartache from breaking up, you would have to be falling in love every other month to revive the initial cocktail in your head. The neurotransmitters and hormones in the quantities that make one feel infatuated are distributed only at the beginning of the relationship. I think we can agree that finding different strategies to optimize your brain is a better option instead.

I have been fascinated by the human brain for as long as I can remember. I felt that there was some little thing different about my brain. Some things that applied to my friends did not apply to me. For example, I always had a hard time focusing on the words in songs and remembering what each song was about. I cannot hold my attention to lyrics. The chorus helps, but that is all I can remember after the song has been repeated so often that nobody wants to hear it anymore. This was not an issue for me until I became a mother and my husband started pointing out I should not let our daughter listen to some songs due to their explicit content.

A couple of other interesting things about my brain that are different include seeing dates on a 'wheel' whenever I think about a particular month or someone's birthday and viewing sentences as a kind of mathematical equation. I see the structure of language in a way that others do not. This really helped me to learn new languages effortlessly.

Some words have a feeling about them. Some are nice, some can be painful. Sometimes the way a word feels has truly little to do with its actual meaning. For example, the word disaster feels like a firework. It took me four decades to learn that I have synesthesia, a condition where two or more senses combine. Synesthesia is individual to each person, but there are similarities.

Some people with synesthesia can see words in colors or see colors in music as it plays. The most common form has to do with the spatial arrangements of dates, like in my case. You can also feel a physical sensation about a word, which, in my case, does not apply to all words. Most of the time, I can go about my day without being tickled or hurt by a conversation. To me, words have enormous power. I am quite sure that it played a role in me becoming an author. I can write in a way I find soothing.

There is no organ in your body that is more unique than your brain. Do not let anyone tell you that their method is guaranteed to work for you. Keep that in mind throughout this book. Not everything may apply to you. But, since we are all humans, I would suggest evaluating the techniques in this book and, if you are healthy enough, giving them a try.

Chapter 1

Every Brain is Unique

"The mind has a mind of its own."

Author unknown

"This morning at 7:15, Mom was hit by a car while she was crossing the road. She was transported by helicopter to Motol hospital in Prague. She has fractured her skull and pelvis…"

I woke up to this bizarre message from my sister on December 28th, 2016, halfway around the world in Oregon. It did not seem possible. If it were true, wouldn't she have called me? But this was not something she would joke about. I called my sister hoping this was some kind of mistake. It was not.

Our mom was in the hospital, her condition uncertain. There was bleeding in her brain and no one knew when, or if, she was going to pull through. But it was not only the injuries from the accident that gave the doctors concern. When my mom was just twenty years old, she had brain surgery, which now made everyone less certain about her recovery. The doctors said that the next three days would be critical to her survival.

What could I do? Sit for three days on standby? Try to find three connecting flights (which would be almost impossible at the end of the year) and spend one full day traveling back?

I began searching for flight tickets. It took me until January 1 to make it there, due to a severe snowstorm that canceled one of my flights. I welcomed the New Year of 2017 somewhere over Greenland. No one on the plane announced it, as though this holiday was cursed for everyone around me as well.

My mom survived those three critical days in the hospital and had a day of lucidity with me. Then she slowly started to forget nouns in her speech. After that, it was verbs and later even names. But she was here. We were all beginning to understand that the brain damage was possibly too severe to ever have our brilliant mom back. But she lived. That is what mattered in the end.

Why had this happened? Just two weeks before my mom's accident, I had decided to write a book that would follow my first, *Hear Your Body Whisper*. My readers were asking for more, so I resolved to write about the brain. Was it a cruel joke? Was my muse messing with me to make me dig deeper into the subject of the brain?

I have always been interested in the brain, and I just started a practice that was supposed to rewire my thinking path. I planned to focus on exploring neuroplasticity and options that are available to everyone – such as meditation, crossword puzzles, and downloading mentally stimulating games on the phone. I had not planned to start studying the physical structure of the brain and question what is truly possible and understand why some people are not able to use these techniques.

I could not start on this book back then – the reality was too painful for that. But I did dive into studying the brain with an obsessive drive, as if I could find something that would help me save my mom. I found new ways of testing. But unfortunately, those options were not only unavailable in the Czech Republic, but still unknown. Even so, that did not mean that knowing more about her condition would help with any kind of treatment.

Sadly, I could not stay with her for long. I had a life and family in Oregon that I needed to return to. I began making arrangements so that I could visit my mom and stay in my home country longer.

For four months, she never left the hospital bed waiting for me to make it there. She passed within fifteen minutes of my arrival. Both of her daughters by her side. In her condition, it did not seem possible for her to hold life inside. I realized I was granted the biggest honor of my life, to be there during the magical moment of my mother's transition to the other side.

I wrote this book to honor my mom. She was the second person in the Czech Republic to have brain surgery. She lived a full life until the age of 77, when she passed due to the cumulative effects from this accident. In the 57 years between her brain surgery and brain trauma after the car accident, she received not one but two Ph.D.'s, and her mind was one of the most fascinating ones I have ever encountered.

Every person's brain is unique, more so than any other organ. While training methods can be generalized and applied successfully on a healthy brain, when the brain starts to suffer, generalized techniques often do not work. Until the root of the problem is understood, any kind of medication or therapy is just shooting darts in the dark hoping to hit the target.

Even the same brain may not react the same way at different times of life. This was the case with my mom who made it through being weeks in a coma as a young adult, having a brain surgery at that time and still returning to a normal life. Yet the last brain injury was fatal later in her life.

The new science of neuroplasticity is giving amazing results to improve the human brain at any point in life. We are no longer bound by those old beliefs that we are born with a certain number of neurons which die during the course of a person's life. This is something you hear all over popular magazines and from life coaches.

In this book, we will critically examine some of these techniques and understand the logical reasons behind them. To understand how your brain is unique, we need to talk about common structure as well.

The next chapter is dedicated to the basic structure of the brain and can be referred to throughout the book. There is no organ in your body that can adapt and change so much to fit different needs, while also being so sensitive to the slightest malfunctioning in some of its areas. While I want to stress that your brain is distinct and amazing in every way, let us also look into how similar it is in the animal and human kingdom.

Chapter 2

Basic Structure, Function, and Communication

"The human brain has 100 billion neurons, each neuron connected to 10 thousand other neurons. Sitting on your shoulders is the most complicated object in the known universe."

Michio Kaku

It would be hard to talk about the brain if we didn't know at least the basics of its structure. In this book, there will be references to some sections of the brain which, along with a basic understanding of brain anatomy, will help clear up some mysteries.

To begin with, you should know that every animal has some form of a brain. Scientists think that brains developed in the animals because of movement. Across all animals, one similarity is that the brain has four parts. How those four parts look depends on the evolution of each respective animal group.

Apparently to us humans, the size of the brain matters and we brag about it a lot. But humans do not have the largest brain – that distinction belongs to the sperm whale. But we do have the largest cerebral cortex relative to the size of our brain. This is what makes us the most intelligent life-form on the planet with the capacity to think like no other animal.

The first part of the brain is not the brain itself, but it is always counted as a part of the brain. This is the **spinal cord**. It is followed by the **hindbrain**, **midbrain**, and **forebrain**.

Across all animal species, the brain evolved from those four parts and still has them in some form. In more primitive life forms, they are still somewhat in a straight line while in humans or dolphins they sort of erupted over themselves. It may surprise you to know that every human goes through this evolution in their life. As a fetus, your brain and nervous system develop from a very primitive looking brain structure.

The functions start with the spinal cord, where the most

basic survival functions are stored. For example: breathing, heart beating, and other organ and system functions.

Reflexes are stored here as well. For instance: when your hand gets burned, the instinctive need to pull it away from the heat comes from your spinal cord. This quick response to stimuli happens to protect the body quickly by allowing the information to travel to the brain without having to go any extra distance. The thinking part of the brain is informed as you reflectively remove the hand, after which it delivers the feeling of pain.

The thinking part of the brain is on the other side of the four parts I mentioned earlier. It is the largest part of the human brain which looks like a swollen walnut. More primitive body functions – and also the most crucial ones for survival – are stored closer to the spine. The more difficult and abstract the functions are, the further away they'll be from the spinal cord.

In humans, those four parts evolved and are called the brainstem, cerebellum, thalamus, and cerebrum.

Brainstem is made up of three parts called medulla oblongata, pons, and midbrain. All functions are dire to our survival. Here you reflexively respond to harmful stimuli as well as make sure your organs work as I mentioned above. Any damage to the brainstem is catastrophic. .

Cerebellum lies just behind the brainstem, in the part just above the back of your neck. This part of the brain is responsible for your movement and memory associated with movement. Thank your cerebellum for being able to ride a bicycle after not riding one for decades. I find adding movement to things I want to remember to be a huge help to my cerebellum where the information would be stored.

Thalamus is located in the central part of the brain, just above the brainstem and cerebellum and beneath each cerebral hemisphere. Such position calls for function worthy of it. The thalamus is sort of a hub that sorts the information based on what needs to be done with it. Almost all sensory information goes through here.

Just below the thalamus is a smaller structure called **Hypothalamus**. The location is roughly above the roof of your mouth. This is responsible for the regulation of temperature, your circadian rhythm, etc. What's more important from the perspective of this book is to understand that this is where the **pituitary gland** is situated.

Continuing the analogy of the brain having its own bar to send out cocktails, the fun-sounding pituitary gland is the distillery of the brain. It is here where most hormones are created. And even those hormones that are created in other glands are in most cases controlled by the pituitary gland. To give you an unforgettable visual, the pituitary gland looks like miniature testes, which it also happens to control. This tiny pea-sized part of the brain holds the key answer to the title of this book.

Cerebrum is that part of the brain that everyone imagines when we say the word brain. No wonder, since it takes up about 85% of the brain. Those chubby walnut-like halves are a magical place for thinking. This is where humans outperform other animals. In the Cerebrum, we make sense of information sent in. We ponder life and make complex strategies.

The cerebrum is made up of the left and right hemispheres. The bridge connecting them together is called the **corpus callosum**. We tend to process certain things on one side and other things on the other side of the brain. I am sure that you have heard that before but what is interesting about this is the plasticity of the cerebrum. Your brain is always ready to learn. In the event of an unfortunate situation, functions of one side of the brain can be acquired by the other side if necessary. Sometimes doctors disconnect the brain's hemispheres, usually to stop seizures in patients without making a noticeable difference in a patient's life. Even if one half of the hemispheres is entirely taken out, the other half can take on all the functions of the removed one without anyone noticing changes in the character of the person.

The outer layer of the cerebrum is called the **cerebral cortex**. The cerebrum has white and grey matter. The easiest description of the cerebral cortex is that it consists of gray matter and constitutes about 80% of the whole brain.

The cerebral cortex is further broken down into specific lobes and other specific cortex areas, such as the frontal cortex where most complex thinking happens. Or the orbital cortex where scientists believe emotions are born and where psychopaths show little to no activity under functioning magnetic resonance imaging. I will talk about these in detail a little more as the book progresses.

Now that we have covered the physical structure and basic functions of the brain, let us look at the way these parts communicate.

The brain has two types of brain cells – neurons and the lesser-known glia. Neurons are the superstars of the brain while glial cells are known for being the filler. For a long time, there was no function given to them. To this day, the word glia is plural and there is no singular word for those cells. However, glial cells have recently been getting attention and recognition because these cells communicate as well as neurons, although in a different way.

When neurons want to send out thoughts or information on how to react to a presented situation, they use synapses. A synapse is a structure at the end of the neuron that allows the passage of information. There are two kinds of synapses: an electrical synapse and a chemical synapse. As you can imagine, in electrical synapses the information passes like lightning and is almost as fast. In a chemical synapse, the information must pass a membrane using a neurotransmitter that is capable of such a job.

There are three kinds of neurotransmitters: excitatory, inhibitory, or modulatory. Excitatory neurotransmitters give rise to an electrical signal called action potential in the receiving neuron while the inhibitory transmitter prevents it. It depends on the receptor the neurotransmitter binds to whether it is excitatory or inhibitory.

Modulatory neurotransmitters are a bit different. They do not rely on the synapse and can affect a large number of neurons at once. They regulate the number of neurons and operate slower than excitatory and inhibitory neurotransmitters.

The strongest synaptic connection is more likely to repeat. The more that the connection repeats, the more likely it is to repeat again and again. And as for you, the conscious mind, it becomes harder to fight against it.

When you experience something for the first time, a new connection is likely to happen. When the experience is extremely intense, it can override the preexisting connection and change the way you are going to react to the situation.

For example: if you have been going to the same restaurant for a long time and you have the same meal each time, you would likely think about having it the next time you go there and your memory of the previous meals would be pleasant. But, if one day you end up with food poisoning, the next time you think of that dish you will not have a pleasant feeling and it is unlikely you would want to eat the same dish at the same restaurant again.

When I think about creating new connections, I imagine them like drops of water trickling down from the top of a hill.

As the drops find their way down, they start to form a groove in the hill. More and more drops pick the same groove until it becomes deep enough to make a riverbed. If an intense experience happens then, instead of just drops, it is like a bucket of water has been poured on that hill. Sometimes the groove may not be enough, so it creates a new one.

This is a scenario that generally happens without our conscious permission. We only become aware of this when this riverbed is messing up our lives. So, what can we do? It is not easy to change that groove, as the drops of water want to come down the same way. We can create an intense experience that overrides this groove, though this is not always possible, especially if we are expecting it. The element of surprise is almost always needed to create a new connection. The event needs to have a strong emotion behind it. If you ever attended Tony Robbins' seminars, you know that this is how he changes people over the course of a few days. This can be difficult to do on your own, but you can use this to help others, like your spouse or a child. That said, you must be careful not to cause more damage.

Throughout this book, we will investigate how to get back in control.

As you can see, there are parts of the brain that are plastic and we can affect them a lot while there are parts that are sensitive to the slightest amount of damage without a good chance of repair. When it comes to healing or improving the brain, it depends on the area of the brain as well as on the individual. To this day, not much can be claimed with absolute certainty.

Chapter 3

How Is a Thought Born?

"Start each day with a positive thought and a grateful heart."

Roy T. Bennett

How is a thought born? I never could have imagined how difficult it would be to answer that question. The honest truth is — we do not know. We, as humans, can speculate, but we cannot pin it down. There is no clear definition of 'thought'; Wikipedia has over a dozen, which makes answering this question that much more difficult.

Generally, you come across two main streams of thought. The first is that thoughts come from ideas that flow through the universe and, in some divine way, enter our mind. The second one places the birth of thought in the brain, as a result of electrochemical reactions between the complex highway of billions of neuropathways. But when we physically send electromagnetic impulses to the brain, we cannot create thoughts artificially.

Personally, I think that the truth lies somewhere in between. However, since this book is about the brain, we will focus on the brain as the vessel for ideas flowing around us.

For a moment, let us visit philosophers of ancient Greece. What do ancient Greek philosophers have to do with the concept of thoughts? A lot, if you allow me to sidetrack for a moment. To me, and in many online dictionaries, the closest synonym to a thought is an idea.

The word "idea" comes from Plato. According to Plato's theory, there is a world of ideas where everything already exists in its "ideal" form. Those ideas exist around us and materialize in the world that we know. However, this is only one perspective. There is no question that the ancient philosophers made an incredible impact on the world and our way of thinking.

We have limited access to our thoughts. The ideas brought into this world from our awareness of things around us can later be materialized into actual matter. Everything in this world needs matter and form to be created. Your thoughts are messengers that carry in the potential for manifestation.

Just like how you can only see the tip of the iceberg above water, you are aware of only ten percent of your thoughts. However, all thoughts have the power to manifest themselves. Since thoughts are born in our brains and our brains are the headquarters for our wellbeing, anything can be manifested in your body without you being aware of the reason.

Being in control of your thoughts is a huge advantage for anything in life. But to be honest, it will not be the only thing needed. Aside from those elusive ideas floating around and through us, we also have the material body with the imperfect, yet still awe-inspiring, brain. The brain can support or suppress these thoughts with various chemical cocktails.

While this chapter had a philosophical base, we will focus on tangible studies of the brain in the following chapters to develop a perfect cycle between our thoughts and the brain.

As an example of what you are capable of achieving, think of the last time you were in love, or thought you were in love. You can likely remember how your thoughts were happier in general, and not just when you were daydreaming about the object of your affection. Those feelings were due to the chemical cocktail made with a mixture of neurotransmitters and hormones in your brain, which we will examine in chapter 10. By removing some of the mystery behind this special bar, you will be able to implement adjustments in your life to be in a better control of your life's focus.

Chapter 4

Can the Body Heal the Brain?

"There's a lot of neuroscience now raising the question, 'Is all the intelligence in the human body in the brain?', and they're finding out that, no, it's not like that. The body has intelligence itself, and we're much more of an organic creature in that way."

Joel Kinnaman

When I moved to the United States in my late twenties, my life changed drastically. It was not the move itself that affected me, but the difference in lifestyle. I had lived in three countries on two different continents prior, so it did not initially seem like anything out of the ordinary. However, in a small town in the high mountain desert of Oregon, it was not easy for me, as a foreigner, to find friends among the descendants of the Wild West cowboys. But I did find the nature breathtaking and the people tough. I admired both – and still do.

When I turned thirty, I gave birth to my beautiful daughter overseas and returned with her to my home in Oregon. While I was over the moon to have a baby, I was beyond exhausted. My daughter had the worst case of separation anxiety. She would not allow me to put her down for more than a second during the first eight months of her life. She would not even allow my husband to hold her.

I was homebound, doing the same thing over and over. Most of my time was spent reading about raising a baby, rarely ever talking to other adults for weeks at a time. There were no grandparents to help and I had no friends to talk to. My husband was working and, when he got home, we were both exhausted. The only conversations I could hold were about our baby. Thankfully, she learned to crawl at eight months, and that got her excited to start exploring, improving her separation anxiety.

However, I was still not used to the lack of sleep. I was interrupted every three hours for nursing, changing the baby, and then trying to fall back asleep only to get up two hours later. This repeated for the first three years with the precision of a Swiss watch. The exhaustion eventually led me to developing acute health issues, with a fever raging so high that my brain was in danger.

My focus began to fade away after a few years. I was just a barely functioning mom, trying to do things with my daughter, but even simple baby crafts took a lot out of me. Despite that, I did have a blast being a mom especially when our daughter became a toddler. Sometimes, I even think my brain regressed to the level of a toddler during this time.

I read that nursing temporarily lowers a mother's IQ and raises her intuition, as it is important during the early childhood of the baby for this to happen. I have no idea if this information is factual, but it seemed true in my case. I nursed for four and a half years and lived a very solitary life. I was so fatigued that I could not even try to drive to the city for activities. In a way, I settled for this life. And, as my daughter grew older, I homeschooled her.

It was not all bad. I was eating quality organic food and my body was strong, especially after being so exhausted for such a long time. If you have any friends or family who have become new parents, think of what they are going through. And, even if all you can offer is your company, go and say "Hi" to them. For me, since I had no one other than my husband, and talking to my body is my specialty, I decided to ask for help with my brain.

Gurus are quite divided on how to achieve this. Some say it

is through your body; others say it is with nutrition, though this process is slower. I personally do not think one is better than the other. While nutrition is, without a doubt, important, the body responds to other stimuli just as much, if not more.

How do you get those results then? Physical exercise and meditation are the go-to methods, as you might expect, but there are other activities as well. The combination of these activities, life choices (depending on your situation), and nutritional intake will help make this process easier. In this chapter, let us look quickly at the two cornerstones: meditation and exercise.

Meditation, for this purpose, is done best when laying down with your eyes closed and focusing inward. Not just on your breath, although that is a start, but on your body. If you would like in-depth instructions, you can download this meditation for free on my website: www.otakaraklettke.com/meditation

This meditation was written with the intent for you to record it using your own voice and adjust it to your exact needs. It focuses on healing your body and the problems you may be facing or needing to address. After you feel the connection with your body to be true to you, you can begin making requests to heal your body or help your brain. You can do this by focusing on allowing the desired neurochemicals to be released by your brain. We will focus on the actual cocktail that your brain can make in Chapter 10.

A majority of your brain cells are used, primarily, to control the functions of your body. Using your body as the means of communication with your brain is like asking your best friend (which your body should be) to talk to their mother for you. The brain is responsible for all the functions that are performed by the organs of your body non-stop throughout your entire life.

According to the famous professor of psychology, Jordan Peterson, the cerebellum has the highest number of neurons compared to any other part of the brain. We do not really know why. The cerebellum seems to mostly be responsible for keeping us on our feet, keeping us balanced, and coordinating muscle movement. It is an ancient part of our brain, and yet it seems difficult for us to wrap our minds around the idea that this part of the brain (which is consistent across all animals) is so dense with neurons.

Similarly, the rest of our brain is mostly configured to operate our entire body. As much as we want to give credit to the newer parts of the brain (in an evolutionary sense) that humankind seems so proud to possess, the prefrontal cortex does not have that many neurons. So, depending on the perspective, we can view it as the young and unexperienced part of our brain that comes up with new or complex ideas. But it does not have the wisdom of the old brain, which has already been developed and is working at its best.

As you can see, the strongest connection of your brain is with your body and not as much with your mind. That is why the best way to hear the whispers of your brain is through the parts that communicate with your body.

To conclude the question in the heading of this chapter, yes, the body can heal the brain. The body has the best relationship with your brain and the effects coming from your body are the longest lasting.

Chapter 5

Improving Your Brain

"There is no scientific study more vital to man than the study of his own brain. Our entire view of the universe depends on it."

Francis Crick

What is the secret? What is your brain trying to whisper to you about improving itself? I would rather answer this at the end of this book, after I have gotten a chance to get into the scientific nitty-gritty. But I know that many of you reading this book are busy and anxious to read it now – I know I always am when I read a book intending to learn something.

In that respect, I will devote the rest of this book to helping you find your own recipe. But, in this chapter, I will offer a quick explanation on what I do to improve brain functions as well as what helps me reach this state of flow more often. I am going to spill the basics of what will be explained in the following chapters. I highly encourage you to read on after this segment, as there will be information that will make this chapter clear from a scientific standpoint. That, in return, should help you to reinforce all the things mentioned here.

You do not have to do them all, and you may find something else that works wonders outside of this book. As neuroscientist Arne Dietrich told me, "Every person is different, and everyone's brain will respond to different stimuli. There is no single recipe."

You have to learn the needs of your brain yourself. Think of this chapter as my speedy recommendation for those that are too busy to read the whole book, or who need a sample of what will be coming up in greater detail and from a fun scientific perspective.

The most important thing for every brain is sleep. There is no unique exception to any brain of any living being on this planet. You may not die from a lack of sleep, but your brain will not function well without it. It is easy to put sleep on the back burner to gain a few extra hours, but without sleep, your brain cannot clean toxins, put learned skills and information into the long-term memory, or keep the body healthy. If you want to improve your brain, my first advice would be to make sure you get at least seven hours of quality sleep (this could be more for certain people and age groups).

Exercise is, based on my research, the second-most important thing for the brain. Unlike sleep, this is way more individual in its effects. For me, this means cardio-intensive dancing. It is important to get the heart rate up and bring more oxygen to the brain. I discuss this in detail in a separate chapter as well. Make sure you visit Chapter 17 to know more.

Also, most certainly go to https://otakaraklettke.com/exercise to check out my free video about the brain power exercise! In that video, you can experience a combination of powerful techniques that focus specifically on increasing positive neurotransmitters in your brain and allowing the creation of new neural pathways.

If you could take one thing from this book to change your life for the better, start every morning with this exercise. Your FREE access is https://otakaraklettke.com/exercise.

Meditation is another thing I use to maintain brain fitness; however, this is not something that works for everyone, or is possible for everyone to do. While many people benefit from meditating, I understand that there are people who simply cannot drop into, or maintain, a meditative state, even if they have been trying for a long time.

If you are one of those people, do not feel bad, and simply find something that is similar and works for you. I would still encourage you to check Chapter 18 to understand better what meditation does to your brain. This may help you get the know-how, though I do have alternate suggestions coming up.

During meditation, the frequency of your brain slows down. With training, an individual can learn how not to become affected by sensory input. But, if someone suffers from ADHD, or has some other reason that prevents the brain from being constantly on alert, meditation can be a difficult task.

In such cases, taking away sensory input can lead to the same or similar results. Sensory deprivation tanks, also known as isolation tanks or floatation tanks, can be the solution for such circumstances.

They are filled with an extremely salty solution, which offers full buoyancy. This liquid is the same temperature as the skin, and so is the air within the tank. When one enters the tank, stimuli like light or sound are gone. And by floating in water that is the same temperature as the skin, one feels like being inside a dream.

Sensory deprivation is a highway to meditation. By reducing sensory input, the brain has nothing to do, so it resets itself like in meditation. Except this time, it does not matter if the person experiencing this does not know how to meditate. Having said that, meditation obviously helps to deepen the effects of the tank.

I wanted to test the effects of a sensory deprivation tank on myself. So, for about six months, I floated once per week. Every experience seemed a little different and I could never predict the outcome of the float, but they were all positive.

The first time I floated was my favorite. Soon, my ninety-minute sessions felt about twenty minutes long. I was never able to judge time in there. When I left my first session, I felt more connected to the "now" than I'd ever felt before. In that moment, I was experiencing the strongest connection to the world around me.

I remember being awestruck over fall leaves and my husband talking to me about something that was not relevant to the moment. So, I refused to let his words reside in my head. I just let them pass through me (do not tell him that though). My interest lay in the cloudy skies and spotty sunlight, the smell of the fall air, and the breeze moving with us. The trees, people, cars, and buildings… it all seemed so much more intense and captivating. I felt like I was a part of everything around us. This was due to my prefrontal cortex having been turned off in the tank and slowly coming back to its ever-thinking self.

Despite having initially come in feeling grumpy just like every other person, in a few months, I was leaving the place with a grin on my face. It seemed like half the time I would either fall asleep or enter some sort of similar headspace. Sometimes I would go in with a specific problem I would try to find a solution for, but I was rarely able to think over serious matters. As if there was a voice in my head that would say, "Not now. Now you are here to decompress." And I would just empty my mind.

Floating was not only beneficial to my mind but my body as well. The salty water supported my body in a way that allowed it to float and provide true physical relaxation for my muscles. This is not like sleeping. When you are in bed, you are touching the bed. So, it is sometimes difficult to tell where the tension is in your body. This is different when you are floating.

I was instantly aware of the areas I was keeping my stress in. In my case, it was my neck and most of my torso. Floating facilitated an instant awareness about this. Just the awareness alone made me loosen up my muscles. Every float felt like a massage (though, even during normal massages, I was still holding tension in my body). Additionally, the psychological boost I got plus the price of floating made this better than paying for any other alternative that could produce the same results.

I understand that some people are afraid to enclose themselves in total darkness and feel no gravity or temperature. After a few minutes, you are not aware where water ends and air begins. This is the most common complaint people share when I encourage anyone to give floating a try. You can always start with the door open above you and the light on. Eventually, you will get there. Sometimes, people do not get the amazing first experience that I did and need a second session for that. So, if you have never tried, give floating a shot!

Besides floating, fasting is another practice I incorporated into my life to benefit the brain. It is one of the few things you can do to stimulate the growth of new neurons. Let us face it. We humans, as a species, are not capable of outrunning animals, nor do we have special hunting skills without the use of tools. We survived throughout history because some of us were able to outsmart the situation and then taught these skills to others.

When you fast, your body's first instinct is to tell you to eat. Survival kicks in. It makes you hungry. Starving. But after about two days, the hunger goes away and you gain clarity. Your brain is doing what we do better than any other creature on this planet – it wants you to think your way out of the hunger. Your brain gets a boost and your body becomes surprisingly energized.

Historically, fasting was a noble practice of kings and religious followers, or as a means of peaceful protest. It creates a space for deepening meditation, which has been the most common reason to fast. Hippocrates, the father of medicine, had all his patients fast before implementing any treatment or medication. He believed that fasting would allow the body to heal itself. In many primitive cultures, fasting was required before going to war or hunting. Major religions call for fasting at least once per year.

Today, fasting is gaining popularity again. There are multiple ways people fast. The strictest method is 'Dry Fasting'. That means consuming nothing at all. Not even water. I have never done that, so I asked my friend Michael about it, who fasts more than anyone I know.

To my surprise, he manages dry fasting for about six days straight while maintaining a full-time job as a semi driver. By all reasoning, he should probably be dead. But instead, he slowly moves from dry fasting to water fasting and can keep going with water for about a month. He claims he does it just so he can see what his body is capable of. Generally, people who practice dry fasting do it to heal inflammation in the body, as bacteria and inflammation need water to exist.

I personally prefer water fasting, which is where I drink salty water to keep minerals in my body. In the end, I fast to grow neurons and not to heal inflammation. Without the salt, I get headaches as, during fasting, the body loses minerals and adding a little bit of salt with high mineral content fixes this problem.

At this point, I am hungry only occasionally after the first day of fasting, now that my body has become used to it. I feel like the clarity in my head and my immune system has gotten stronger. Just like Hippocrates started his patients with fasting, I lower my food intake whenever I feel something is trying to get me. When I fast, I feel invincible. Apparently, I also become more effective when splitting logs. As if my body is getting stronger without the food. I like to fast for three to five days to feel the benefits.

In 2018, I fasted for five days every three months. I am not sure if I got smarter that year, but I know I did not have a single cold – not even a tiny one. I still fast about as often; however, I shortened my fasts to three days as I do not mind doing them in more frequent intervals.

Full fasting is not for everyone. It was not for me either. I have a liver condition where, if I do not eat, I start throwing up until I pass out. Sometimes I pass out before, which is much nicer. So, my first fasting experience took a lot of meditation and speaking to my liver. I did manage to get through it, and my body stopped reacting to not eating for the first time in thirty years.

When it comes to clinical studies of fasting, results have shown exceedingly longer life spans in mice deprived of food than those fed normally. There are many people who fast for the purpose of longevity. I have seen a disturbing video where there was a group of mice with cancer going through treatment. The ones that consumed food died, whereas the ones that were deprived of food went on to beat cancer.

Some people choose intermittent fasting as an "easier" alternative to full fasting. In this method, one eats only during a set number of hours (usually eight or fewer) and then does not eat for the remaining hours of the day. People claim to see the same benefits as with full fasting.

I, however, was not feeling the results even after one full month of intermittent fasting. I did find it beneficial, but not for the brain quality that I wanted. I was not any faster at solving cognitive problems after prolonged periods of intermittent fasting compared to any other time. On the third day, and directly after water fasting, I was solving logical puzzles much faster than on the non-fasting days.

Most of the research on fasting was conducted in the former Soviet Union, during the Cold War. It was a cheap solution to many problems. Unfortunately, that knowledge did not get out until much later, and to this day I am not aware if the results of those studies were published in other parts of the world.

While there is a lot of information available on fasting, it was hard for me to find many backed by true scientific data. For that reason, I feel it's best to share my personal experience with fasting which is very subjective of course. Even so, I fast with a group of people, so I was able to talk to increase the sample size and all of us share amazing and similar benefits when it comes to fasting.

If you have never fasted and are interested in starting, there are a few tips I have for you. First of all, make sure you are healthy enough to go through this. For example, people with diabetes should not fast. When you are beginning your fast, do not stress about hunger and do not avoid looking at food. If you get hungry, imagine eating whatever feels like a great snack. Imagine every bite.

Interestingly, if a person is avoiding food it makes them want it more. The hunger and desire to eat gets stronger. But, if you imagine the taste and the structure of food in your mouth, you can trick your body into feeling the sensation of eating and the hunger will go away. I do not know why, but I always seem to imagine eating German chocolate cake (though I never actually do). Just the feeling of eating dense, sweet chocolate is satisfying. I hope you can give fasting a try.

Moving on to sunlight. Yes, this is about vitamin D, but even more so about spending time outdoors and in the actual light itself. It is critical to our mental health that we are exposed to these conditions. Even prisoners get their daily dose of light and fresh air. It would be inhumane otherwise.

Exposure to sunlight is connected to the production of serotonin. If we do not get enough serotonin, we can get depressed. Outside air, especially around water with lush foliage and forest, is filled with essential oils and phytoncides. These are volatile organic compounds emitted by trees and plants. They prevent the growth of attacking organisms. Air, near water, is filled with negative ions that are natural antidepressants. Take your next hike along the river and enjoy the sunshine!

Surround yourself with good people! Based on a study that has been in progress for about 100 years at Harvard University, the biggest factor in longevity is not what you eat or how you exercise, but who you spend your time with.

Interaction with the outside world matters, and if we have a prominent person in our lives, it is important that we are happy with that person since they are the one we spend most of our time with.

If there is no such person, then they are replaced by those we meet in life – our friends, and even the cashier at the store who asks how our day is going. Humans are social creatures, even the introverted ones. It is not about how much time we spend socializing, but the quality of the socialization.

Play stimulating brain games! Yes, crossword puzzles and Tetris are beneficial for your brain. Many computer games can be too, despite popular belief. I was not a fan of computer games until I read up on some studies regarding the subject. This does not mean that doing puzzles will save you from Alzheimer's, or not doing so will condemn you, but it is a solid brain exercise that has long-term benefits. However, once your brain gets the hang of it, there is no benefit to it. So you need to keep switching games or increasing the difficulty.

Basically, whenever you are doing things out of habit, and you are not consciously engaging with the action, it helps to do something else that will make you focus on what you are doing in the moment. Keep challenging your brain. Simple things like brushing teeth with your non-dominant hand can help you form new neural pathways in your brain.

Of all the suggestions listed above, the intent is to induce a state of flow. This magical state of our brain lets us do better than we would under normal circumstances. I am grateful that I had a chance to interview neuroscientist Arne Dietrich who first described this state of the brain and gave it its scientific name "transient hypofrontality." You can read about it in detail in Chapter15.

We will talk about the brain in much more detail in the following chapters. We will look at the drugs the brain makes and those legal ones we choose to add. We will talk about fun stuff, like sex, as well as the not so fun stuff, like serious problems in the brain. In all, I hope you will choose to keep reading this book as the most fascinating things are still to come!

Chapter 6

Accessing the Subconscious Mind

"To shift your life in a desired direction, you must powerfully shift your subconscious."

Kevin Michel

The majority of human functions are accomplished automatically, using the subconscious mind or the oldest part of the brain. The conscious mind operates only that which we are aware of, while the subconscious mind handles the rest. It is a cognitive mechanism that keeps us on autopilot most of the time. Depending on which scientific article you find, we are consciously in control only about 2-10% of the time.

Sigmund Freud separated the mind into three parts. Besides the conscious and subconscious mind, he also speaks about the unconscious mind. The unconscious mind is where the skeletons in our closets reside. Here, traumatic experiences that you forced yourself to forget about are stored. That said, your body and brain will still act based on the information stored there when presented with a trigger, such as smell, sound, or visual stimuli.

The conscious mind (in other words, you or me) can speak with the subconscious mind. The closer you are to your consciousness, the better the odds for communicating with your conscious mind.

Like a farmer on a ranch, you would not have the time to direct everything yourself. It is similar to how a farmer needs many ranch hands to make sure all the creatures are tended to, which is what the unconscious mind does for you. Those ranch helpers – in other words, your unconscious mind – carry out orders like the microorganisms in your body do.

Human cells are only ten percent of the entire human body. Mostly we are bunch of viruses, bacteria, even fungi, all living on the planet human. Your mind is the leader. No worries, you are the ultimate one in charge. You decide to take your body to work and sometimes let the subconscious take over during the routine drive on the way there, but when it comes to your consciousness, it is all you.

If you can program your subconscious mind, it will pass a message to your conscious mind and you can ask for what you need – such as healing a certain part of the body. Also, by listening to those microbes, you can address their needs before illness or other problems manifest.

I will not spend time talking about communication with other parts of the body, that was a subject of my first book, but I would like to offer you a free meditation that allows you to whisper to your body at https://otakaraklettke.com/meditation

We need access to the subconscious mind to be able to make positive improvements in our lives. In this book, I am focusing on those things that will help you turn your body into the best farm it can possibly be. I will help you turn your brain into the best bartender it can be for absolute performance. How you choose to use the advice is up to you.

Besides needing to access the subconscious, we also need prevention from the things that are negatively affecting us. These are things such as the TV, news, and advertisements; but may also be your closest family or friends. Ones who may have done something in the past, or are doing something at the moment, that negatively impacts you right now.

The reaction to those stimuli will be the same. And, while change is not impossible, in most cases, it is unlikely. Their behavior is not something you can control, so do not take the blame and do not blame yourself. Blame is your enemy. Blame blocks any new connections between neurons to create a new pathway. We will look at this a little closer in the next chapter. While some triggers are important to work on, for example with people suffering from PTSD, it is practically impossible to address everything that causes triggers.

All these ideas that are placed in our minds affect our bodies, physically and mentally. However, these ideas can be subjective and affect everyone differently, depending on their state of mind at the time. Just ask any set of siblings about their time growing up. Not only will they remember different moments, but their memories will have different emotional energies around the same event. One sibling will remember the event one way, and the other sibling will remember it another way. The way we perceive anything will generate a response in the body.

Our subconscious mind may not seem to be leading the charge, but the conscious mind has no idea what is happening until it hears from the subconscious mind. And it is our external and internal perceptions of the world around us that affect the outcome of our experiences. Just think about placebo pills. They can be powerful enough to heal the patient through the thought the mere thought of being healed alone. Similarly, but on the opposite spectrum, we have the lesser-known nocebo effect.

The nocebo effect is a negative side effect of medication that the patient expects based on the warnings for that medication. Even with placebo healing, there can be negative side effects of sugar pills when the patient is warned about the side effects. If a doctor gives out a medication and tells the patient that she may expect possible vomiting, she is likely to spend some time shouting down the porcelain phone in her bathroom.

As an example, according to MD, author, and TEDx speaker Lissa Rankin, patients who were given a saline solution and told they were receiving chemotherapy started experiencing nausea and even hair loss.

There are several different ways for a person to ensure that the messages they send reach their subconscious mind. In the next chapter, I will look at outer circumstances that affect your brain and mind.

Chapter 7

Subliminal Perception

"The brain is a world consisting of a number of unexplored continents and great stretches of unknown territory."

Santiago Ramon y Cajal

According to the *Collins English Dictionary*, subliminal perception is the "perception of or the reaction to a stimulus that occurs without awareness or consciousness."

Subliminal stimuli is a fascinating subject. When I was in a preparatory high school, I entered an essay competition that involved presenting original research and new ideas on a specific subject. I chose to study and write about advertisement.

At that time, my older sister and her husband were successful at their advertisement agency and it was shocking to see how much the big companies spent to get the attention of potential customers. I created a survey and, in those old pre-internet days, collected almost six hundred detailed answers to my questions. Besides that, I also dove into everything there was to learn about advertisement.

I suspect that it was not everything I had studied that helped me win each round, all the way to the national level, but it was my work on subliminal perception. And of course, it was also the fact that I told the important people in my life (my parents), who thought I was the biggest flake on the planet, that I was going to win the nationals.

The subliminal perception part of my presentation captured everyone's attention. Especially since I used the subconscious minds of the judges against them, I had them fooled before I ever said a word to defend my work.

I named the presentation *Advertisement From A to C* and used a rather romantic font that added a few waves. The font and the way our brains are wired made them think that the title of the presentation was Advertisement From A to Z.

It was a risky move that paid off. Our conscious mind seems to take a huge interest in what we can do to change it. And who else takes better advantage of that than an advertising company?

The history of subliminal advertising goes back to 1957, when a market researcher named James Vicary so famously inserted the words "Eat popcorn" and "Drink Coca-Cola" onto a single frame of a movie which he played in the movie theaters. While the movie viewers did not consciously see anything other than the movie they came to see, their mind had been affected so much that Vicary claimed that Coca-Cola sales went up over 18%, and the popcorn sales by a whopping 57%.

It turned out that his claims were a hoax but, still, this experiment revolutionized advertising and marketing. The effectiveness of subliminal perception was proven later and, in some countries, such manipulation has become illegal. However, proving that someone is toying with another person's mind is practically impossible.

Subliminal messages will manipulate your mind and trick your brain. Do you have any kind of protection against it? Not really, once you are exposed. All you can do is try not to get exposed to begin with. This has its limitations. So, instead of worrying about what it can do to your mind, let us focus on how you could use it to your advantage.

One of the popular ways to access the mind is through affirmations. People use affirmations in hopes of bettering their lives. Interestingly, affirmations work only sometimes and sometimes they make the person more miserable. How is that possible? There are many variables.

For example, if there are negative words that we want to avoid, we end up thinking of them more often. Saying, "I do not procrastinate," can transfer the word "procrastinate" into our subliminal consciousness. Another example would be saying something that you do not believe to be true. The advice, "fake it till you make it," may not work and, in most cases, it does not. You can affirm that you are moving forward and seeing progress in something important to you, but you cannot affirm something if you do not think it is possible. If, however, you believe in your heart (I should say brain really) that whatever you are affirming is in your future and you would do anything to protect that statement, affirmations can do wonders. Just remember to stay positive.

The subconscious mind seems to grab onto keywords. For example, if you say the word "fear," you will experience more fear in your life, even if you use the phrase, "I have no fear". I believe this is a common problem with therapy, where someone continues talking about old wounds over and over. It keeps pushing the same neurosynaptic connection and trying to numb the chemical reaction to it.

Another common piece of advice to trick our subconscious mind is to tell everyone around you that you are getting ready to do some large project, like go on a diet (or in my case writing and publishing a book). I fell victim to it with this very book. I told everyone in the interviews, on social media, and in my life. But, with my mom's accident, I stopped working on it for some time. However, if you are holding this in your hands, it means that I have finally finished it.

To make something stick in our conscious or subconscious mind, we need to really live the experience. This is why sitting behind a school desk and studying by sitting down is actually the complete opposite of how we should study if we want to remember things.

You can form a physical movement pattern or add other senses to the information that you want to transfer into a long-term memory in your subconscious mind. In the end, movement is one of – if not the most powerful – tools to stimulate brain health. You can engage in two different sections of the brain to set something in. This can help override the previous information. Adding other stimuli, such as smell or touch, can help if they can be effectively applied.

So, while your subconscious mind will always do what it wants at any specific moment, your conscious mind can, and even should, prepare for that moment so the subconscious mind comes with a response you desire.

Chapter 8

Intelligence

"Everybody is a genius. But if you judge a fish by its ability to climb a tree, it will live its whole life believing that it is stupid."

Albert Einstein

There are dozens of definitions of intelligence. Intelligence is generally described as the capacity to learn and apply the knowledge or awareness of self, the capability to reason, create art, think abstractly, etc. The one common thing to all definitions is that intelligence has its home base in the brain.

Intelligence has been observed in animals, plants, and even fungi, so we are not the only chosen species on this planet that possesses it. In the book *Are We Smart Enough to Know How Smart Animals Are?* the world-renowned biologist and primatologist Frans de Waal makes a groundbreaking case on animal intelligence.

I am fond of the title itself. Are we, humans, smart enough to be able to judge how smart animals are? Would a squirrel think we are not smart because we cannot bury hundreds of seeds before winter and then dig them out exactly where we buried them months later? While our intelligence should not be compared to that of other species, or even other humans, it can always be compared to the capacity of an individual. Is one more intelligent as a child compared to as a grown adult? Are you more intelligent when you are twenty-five and your prefrontal cortex has finally finished developing, or when you are sixty-five and had a chance to gain life knowledge? The answer depends, again, on the definition of intelligence.

I would like to borrow the Cattell-Horn theory of fluid and crystallized intelligence to give the answer. These psychologists created a concept for two kinds of intelligence. Fluid intelligence is the kind you are born with, something that IQ tests measure. It demonstrates the ability to solve new problems, use logic, and it is independent of learning, experience, or previous practice. On the other hand, crystallized intelligence is based upon experience and prior learning. It is used, for example, in taking tests that are based on the comprehension of previously learned subjects.

As you can guess, fluid intelligence is at its peak during early adulthood and declines with age. Crystallized intelligence, on the other hand, grows with age and peaks around the age of sixty or seventy. So you do not have to feel too bad about aging. Crystallized intelligence is something you can exercise to not only grow, but to protect yourself from cognitive decline.

I will admit that my fear of my brain deteriorating when I reach an old age is something I experience often. What scares me is the fact that, if I am lucky enough to live to my seventies, I can expect that half of my peers will suffer from dementia, Alzheimer's disease, or some other form of degenerative brain disease. The thought that even if I make it, some of my friends will not, and I will have to witness that, scares me.

The research commissioned by Alzheimer's Research UK and carried out by the Office of Health Economics in 2015 set to calculate the probability of Alzheimer's in children born that year. The results were astounding. One-third of the children born that year were expected to develop Alzheimer's at some point in their life. That is not a good prognosis, especially considering that this is only one of a few brain declining conditions.

It is a scary world for today's children to grow up in, but the good news is that the fluid and crystallized intelligence grows and has the potential to grow throughout early childhood and adolescence. As parents, grandparents, or older siblings, we should help kids to increase their intelligence and we should do it with them.

There are many ways we can grow our intellect. First is through physical movement – fast-paced cardio to be exact. And no, you do not have to go crazy with it; you just need 20-30 minutes every other day to feel the effect and to keep the effect long-lasting. You do not need to go to the gym, you can just take your dog on a power walk, or turn up the music and dance while you are cleaning out the dishwasher and doing other household chores.

The point is to move enough to raise your heart rate. I know it does not sound like you are exercising your brain by moving your body, but it is what the brain needs. I promise if you exercise this way for at least a month, you will feel the difference and you will see how your mood and capability to solve problems improves.

Another high-level brain training technique is learning languages. Using a language lights up the brain in many different areas. Pretty much every major lobe is responsible for understanding and using a language. Bilingual children show not only more developed brains or language skills, but also creativity, thinking outside the box, and even mathematical skills. Speaking other languages allows your brain to expand more than doing any other intellectual thing you can do.

The next best thing after learning languages is to play a

musical instrument. You are probably familiar with the concept that music helps the brain but is it unlikely to increase your intelligence. To be fair to those that love listening to music, it is likely to keep your brain healthy and can help it recover after being injured.

Playing a musical instrument makes a firework in the space between your ears. Not only are you listening to music, you are also coordinating your fingers in a fine movement to create the music. This is a great thing to start at any age. If you have little kids, I suggest you find them a good music teacher. Learning to play instruments from a young age is a good option if you are not in a position to raise them bilingually.

After that, there are the common things that everyone seems to know. Doing sudoku, playing neuro-improving games, crossword puzzles, and learning anything in general. The point is that you can improve, at least your crystallized intelligence, at any point in your life. By reading this book, you are already doing a favor to your brain. Can you feel it?

Chapter 9

What Can We Learn from Psychopaths?

"Sentiment is a chemical aberration found on a losing side." – Sherlock Holmes

Sir Arthur Conan Doyle

This chapter is going to be fun. We are going to look at a small group of people whose brain works a little different than most people.

To begin with, I would like to establish the difference

between psychopaths and sociopaths, simply because a lot of people do not know what it is. Psychopaths are born the way they are, with gene combinations that, merged with early life abuse, can create a violent individual with low emotional empathy. In contrast, sociopaths are not ones who are genetically wired for antisocial traits; instead, they are individuals molded from traumatic life circumstances in their youth and end up with antisocial instincts or behaviors.

While prosocial, but not fully antisocial, psychopaths, are often accomplished people in their careers, sociopaths are much more likely to be angry, parasitic, and life leeching on their partners, parents, etc. Although psychopaths often use people around them to get where they want, they do not particularly strive to be parasitic on others.

I had the honest pleasure to interview James Fallon, a famous neuroscientist and professor who, by studying brains of psychopaths, discovered that he was one himself. It truly was a delight talking to him. He is a charming and extremely intelligent person, who is arguably the biggest authority on psychopathy. He is one of the most driven people I have ever met.

To quote Dr.Fallon directly – "Even though basic personality traits are largely determined by genetics, the traits associated with psychopathy are permanently altered 'epigenetically' by trauma or abandonment between birth and two to three years old. Genetic alleles coding for these personality tendencies are passed from both mothers and fathers. However, a key 'warrior' gene (there are about fifteen warrior genes coding for aggression, dominance and competitiveness), the promoter of the MAO-A gene regulating serotonin, is transferred by a gene on the X-chromosome from mothers to children. And since sons only get their X-chromosomes from their mothers, it is the mother who has the largest genetic impact on aggression and violence in their sons. This gene is less likely to impact daughters, therefore, female psychopaths are rarer."

When I asked him about the psychopathic murderers we all know from movies, he said, "In order for the psychopath to become a murderer, he has to have an early serious childhood traumatic event." He had a pleasant childhood, so he focuses on killing his thirst for knowledge, constantly becoming involved in new research all over the world.

I was curious if psychopaths could feel the way others feel and understand other people's feelings. We often hear that they are incapable of feeling sympathy and other feelings related to empathy. Fallon said that psychopaths have cognitive understanding of all those feelings, and, on a cognitive level, they can process empathy. They just do not "feel" it the way we do. I can personally admit that he was charming and interesting, traits that psychopaths are famous for.

In one of the most fascinating books on the subject *The Wisdom of Psychopaths* written by Kevin Dutton, the author not only dissects the brain, but also what we all can learn from them. Most people imagine a serial killer with a charming smile when they hear the word "psychopath". If we were to look at the places where they hang out, it would not be some dark alley waiting for their next victim. They can be found in fancy offices as CEOs, lawyers, politicians, surgeons, or even celebrities. CEOs are the number one profession, according to Dutton, followed by lawyers and TV/Radio people, surgeons, and surprisingly salesmen.

Only an extremely small percentage of psychopaths murder people. It is true that they do not really feel emotions in the way we do, but they do not necessarily crave killing. According to James Fallon, in order to become a killing psychopath, they need to be exposed to actual violence in their childhood. Not just watching it on TV or hearing about it, but experiencing actual first-hand violence.

The brain of a psychopath shows low activity in the orbital cortex, which is towards the center at the base of the frontal and temporal lobes. It is believed that this is the place where our emotions are generated. Maybe because psychopaths do not feel as much as we do, they can observe how emotions play a role in the people around them. This is what makes them great salesmen and many other things. Persuasion is their natural talent because they can analyze what kind of person you are and what works on you.

Specifically, when it comes to surgeons, they are really needed by the rest of society. Just imagine that there is a little child hit by a car who needs a life-saving surgery and the doctor meets the emotionally distressed parents before the immediate surgery. In this case, it is good to have someone who can address this with extraordinarily little emotion. Someone whose pride wants to demonstrate what an amazing surgeon they are.

In all honesty, I would prefer to have a surgery done by a psychopath over someone who can empathize with me. However, this is probably one of very few professions where I found them truly useful. Their God-complex can save lives. It is important to know that psychopaths are always narcissists, however, not all narcissists are psychopaths, so remember that. While they do not make the best partners or parents, they can be valuable to society depending on the field they choose to pursue.

And pursue they will.

The tenacity of psychopaths is remarkable. When they focus on something, they go and get it. They do not mind whoever gets hurt, including them. They have the capacity to block everything else out of their focus for the greater good.

In this way, they can do good for the world. Even someone like Gandhi may have been a psychopath when you analyze his behavior. While Gandhi did amazing work to free the people in India, he was hardly nice to those around him. He even let his own wife die when she was offered antibiotics for her illness, claiming that she could only use Ayurveda and that there was no need for her to use Western medicine. You would think he would claim the same for himself, but no, he took the antibiotics and saved his own life.

However, because he is known for his major works for humanity, he is not known well for how difficult it was for his wife to be close to him or for the naked girls he insisted sleep next to him to prove he was capable of celibacy. I know he is well-loved, and I am well aware that I may have pushed a little too far using Gandhi as an example, but I encourage you to look into his personal life before dismissing what I have said here. The point is that rather than going on a killing spree, psychopaths more often want to be known for something lasting that they will be admired and remembered for. To make a huge political change, or to be the one that brings the world the cure for cancer, this can motivate most psychopaths so much more than getting some joy out of murdering people.

Now do not get me wrong. To allow psychopaths in political offices would be and often is a disaster, as the money could easily make them ignorant of the hatred they cause among the people they are supposed to lead.

What can we learn from them? To focus on a goal. That, when there comes a time when you have a chance to make a difference in the world, it is okay to let your laundry pile up and not cook all your meals from scratch. We learn that we can observe others before we choose the best strategy to talk to them. This is not anything evil, but it is human on many levels.

You know how the same person can be assessed completely differently by different people or groups of people that this person interacts with? It is because only part of our behavior comes from inside us, the other part is simply mirroring others around us.

You know that old grandma that everyone loves, with the smile wrinkles fanning out of the corners of her eyes, who thinks the world of every person, and everyone in her presence just melts? That is a good role model. I get that it is not something we all can be all the time, especially if we still did not earn those smile wrinkles, but we all can take a moment to listen to people first to see who they are and what mood they are in. The simple willingness to be more observant will bring us a little bit more of what comes to psychopaths so effortlessly.

Chapter 10

Brain's Drugs and Functions

"Brain wave tests prove that when we use positive words, our "feel good" hormones flow. Positive self-talk releases endorphins and serotonin in our brain, which then flow throughout our body, making us feel good. These neurotransmitters stop flowing when we use negative words"

Ruth Fishel

I always believed I did not have an addictive nature, until I realized how addicted I am to the drugs that my own brain can generate. I am not alone. There are plenty of people in this world that thrive in the exhilarating moments under dopamine, oxytocin, serotonin, and, not to mention, endorphins, which create socially applauded forms of intoxication of being in love.

In this chapter, I would like to look at some of the most common chemicals that your brain produces, which play a key role in your mood at any given moment.

The way you feel is important for your future and your past, because the way you feel now will be the reason you either repeat or become afraid of feeling a similar way in the future. It will also create a memory for you.

Memories are not a real documentation of the event we lived, rather, they are documentation of the way we felt at that moment. Therefore, the same event can be memorized as traumatic for someone feeling depressed and as beautiful for a person that shared that moment with someone they were falling in love with. We will look at the memory more in-depth in Chapter 12.

Olympic athletes, surfers who get up early to catch the perfect wave, storm chasers, public speakers, or even people who are practicing BDSM for sexual pleasure are, for the most part, addicted to those brain generated chemicals and are willing to risk their lives to get a "high". But, even if you do not thrive in the speed of skiing down the dangerous slopes of the Alps, you may be addicted to the small dose of dopamine that you get with new likes on Facebook.

Little infants get oxytocin from the breast milk, along with other hormones, so in a way we are primed to this addiction from day one. Since those chemicals that are making us feel good are for our health itself, there is hardly ever a reason to stop, unless one is risking their life in hopes of getting more and more adrenaline.

Here is a short list of some of these chemicals. This way, you can come back to this chapter for a quick reference.

Dopamine is one of over one hundred neurotransmitters the brain produces. It basically means that it is a chemical messenger that is released by neurons, which uses synapses as a bridge and then the nerves as a highway to send out messages. The brain creates distinct pathways for dopamine. Dopamine keeps us motivated and promises us a reward in the end. It makes us love life and shows us purpose. People who are serious go-getters are likely to have high doses of dopamine in their bodies. Dopamine keeps us focused on goals.

It is the drug that makes me sit down and work on a book for months for the vision of not only spreading my message, but also for the enormously intoxicating feeling I get every time my book is published. While this was the strongest and lasted for days when I published my first book, I still get the feeling of accomplishment and inner gratitude that feels like it is bursting from inside my body every time I birth a new book.

People who lack dopamine feel no purpose in life and experience a lack of focus and motivation to do anything.

There are things that can be done to boost dopamine naturally, as well as not so naturally, which unfortunately does not help us in the long term. We will look at substances or behaviors that help us and that harm us in the following chapters.

Oxytocin is a hormone released by the hypothalamus. That is the small bottom center portion of the brain. Although most people associate oxytocin with women, because it is commonly associated with childbirth and nursing, it is also produced in males. Both females and males release oxytocin during orgasm, long hugs, cuddling, or social bonding. Women usually have more oxytocin than men, which may be the reason why women are more romantically tuned than men. This love cocktail is made by the master bartender, the pituitary gland.

Oxytocin plays a huge role in our mood. Just because it is known as the "love hormone" does not mean that it is always loving. When a person is in a good mood and good things are happening to them, oxytocin makes the person more trusting and helps to create a positive memory.

However, according to the study done by Northwestern University, this hormone can create traumatic memories and strengthen them. The University concluded that oxytocin is essential for strengthening the memory of negative social interactions and that it increases fear and anxiety in future stressful situations. It seems like we should be careful what situation we find ourselves in when we have heightened levels of oxytocin.

Serotonin is another neurotransmitter, although some scientists believe it is a hormone. Only a small amount is produced by the brain. For the most part, it is produced by our gastrointestinal tract. Since serotonin cannot cross the blood-brain barrier, only the serotonin produced by the brain can be used in the brain itself. Serotonin is sometimes called the "happy chemical", for obvious reasons.

Depression has been linked to low levels of serotonin; however, it is unknown if depression is caused by the low levels, or if depression causes the decrease in serotonin. It also plays a part in our sleep, appetite, sexual desires, and memory. Low levels of serotonin can cause lack of sleep, anxiety, aggression, low self-esteem, and even cravings for sweet or starchy foods.

Endorphins are a whole group of hormones produced by the fun-sounding pituitary gland and by the central nervous system.

Endorphins are basically our "home-made" morphine and opioid. It lowers our pain level and functions with the three chemicals mentioned above to make us feel good.

Pain and stress are the most common factors that produce endorphins, which in return make us feel less pain and less stress. They are also the cause of what is called "runner's high", something athletes are familiar with and is often a huge motivator for training.

Endorphins are also released during sex, especially by those in submissive roles in BDSM practices when they are crossing the pain threshold.

Unlike opioids that are often prescribed by the doctor, I hear that one cannot become addicted to endorphins. Although, I suspect that some athletes are true endorphin addicts.

Ester Ledecka, famous Czech snowboarder and skier and the only woman in the history of the Olympics to earn two gold medals in two disciplines (snowboarding and skiing) during the same Olympic games, is known for her addiction to training.

As her trainer says, "The biggest problem with her is to stop her training at the end of the day." Ester says that all the medals and publicity is just bothering her and, other than sports, she is known to be the ultimate chocolate addict, which increases serotonin and dopamine. I believe she is the example of a happy-brain addict.

Norepinephrine also called **noradrenaline** is a hormone and neurotransmitter. It is synthesized by the body from dopamine by the adrenal medulla, which is not located in the brain, but the brain is the happy recipient of this neurotransmitter.

It plays an important role for the heart and throughout the body. In the brain, it is responsible for our flight or fight response. Norepinephrine makes full evolutionary sense and it likely has played a huge role in our survival as a species.

Have you ever been in a situation where you lost control over your vehicle? That is when norepinephrine would be released. If you've ever experienced it (and I hope it was not serious for everyone involved), you may remember how it felt like time slowed down. Your senses were enhanced, and you were able to process more information than normal. Perhaps you could remember either similar situations from the past or things you have learned to help you in that moment. Your focus was laser-sharp.

If you have ever experienced that, your prefrontal cortex, the part of our brain that we humans are so proud of, changed the activity pattern. Something that may have lasted only a few seconds felt like a lifetime. Norepinephrine may have saved your life. On the other hand, it can cause an anxiety attack, raise blood pressure, and do some harm to your body. Even so, this neurotransmitter has an important place in our lives, but if you are healthy, you do not want to experience high levels too often.

Cortisol is a steroid hormone produced by the adrenal gland. Sometimes, it is referred to as a "stress hormone". Cortisol is not often a good guy. It has many negative effects on the body itself and of course, the brain. A little too much and it can have devastating effects, putting the brain in a state of chronic stress. Something so common in the modern world. This can put the brain in a constant fight or flight state, decrease the number of neurons, and even shrink the brain in size.

Under the leadership of Daniela Kaufer, neuroscientists at the University of California, Berkley, have found that chronic stress can cause long term changes in brain structure and function. Of course, a healthy amount of stress releases just the right amount of cortisol to return to the normal state. If all is well in the body, and there is not too much stress in life, cortisol helps to recover from stress and, under normal conditions, it is helpful to us.

But when too high, it impairs the ability of the brain to function properly. According to Touro University Worldwide, "It can disrupt synapse regulation, resulting in the loss of sociability and the avoidance of interactions with others. Chronic stress has a shrinking effect on the prefrontal cortex, the area of the brain responsible for memory and learning."

GABA is a short name for **gamma-aminobutyric acid** which is another neurotransmitter. This one should be plentiful in all areas of the cortex and throughout the nervous system because its function is to regulate communication between brain cells.

GABA is the kindergarten teacher that makes sure that all the overly excited kids do not get out of hand. It helps us to feel relaxed, brings us to a meditated state, keeps our mood balanced, and aids us with falling asleep. I have heard a couple of independent doctors call GABA "the brakes of the brain" because it takes the brain into a lower gear. By reducing neuroactivity, GABA helps us to calm down and get ready to sleep, reduces mental and physical stress, anxiety, and it is, overall, one of the key helpers in facilitating overall mental and physical balance of the body.

Low levels of GABA can cause stress, anxiety, depression, or simply result in a hard time falling asleep, due to our brain being in overdrive. GABA, along with melatonin, is also one of the natural supplemental sleep aids sold on the market. The good news is that our gut has a huge role in the creation of GABA and, simply eating enough fermented foods like kimchi, sauerkraut, or yogurts, will help increase GABA significantly. Other foods that are helpful are black and green teas, citrus, berries, cocoa, and wine.

Anandamide is a remarkable neurotransmitter produced by the brain. I love its name, which comes from a Sanskrit word *Ananda*, which means "joy, delight, bliss". This chemical compound was discovered by Professor Raphael Mechoulam in 1992. The famous professor from Hebrew University, a couple of decades prior, discovered THC (tetrahydrocannabinol), the chemical found in cannabis that makes people high. He was looking for the body's own chemical for which there were receptors that THC fit into perfectly.

In a simple word, anandamide is our brain's marijuana. Our bodies have their own endocannabinoid system which, according to scientists from Ariel University in Israel, can be detected in the earliest embryonal stages. It oversees development of the brain. Anandamide helps us to feel hungry, for example, but also helps us to regulate stress, save good memories, and protects us from thinking of memories that were not so good. The brain creates anandamide when there is a lot of cortisol to counter stress. People that are naturally happier were found to have higher amounts of anandamide.

The brain has many more neurotransmitters that would be worth mentioning in this book, but I am afraid that if I gave room to all that the scientific community is aware of today, I would have to dedicate a whole book to neurotransmitters alone. Those mentioned above are the biggest heroes, or villains, depending on the individual state of the body.

In the next chapter we will look at drugs and the effect of stimulants that we take in which are not naturally produced by the body.

Chapter 11

This Is Your Brain on Drugs

"People use drugs, legal and illegal, because their lives are intolerably painful or dull. It should tell us something that in healthy societies drug use is celebrative, convivial, and occasional, whereas among us it is lonely, shameful, and addictive. We need drugs, apparently, because we have lost each other."

Wendell Berry

Whether we want to admit it or not, humans love drugs. We love altering our state of consciousness and most of us do it regularly. One well-known drug is the second biggest commodity on our planet, after oil. If you guessed coffee, you are correct! And 99% of coffee drinkers drink coffee for the caffeine. But why? The answer lies in the drug's chemical structure, which is often close to our own chemicals and, in some way, is able to be a lockpick for neuroreceptors. This allows us to release our own drugs that would not be released otherwise, or to be a block in those receptors like in a case of caffeine.

Caffeine is the most common thing we seek for an energy boost or, to be exact, help us from feeling tired and sleepy. According to different studies, up to 90% of adults consume caffeine in some form. Caffeine is found in coffee, tea, chocolate, and many energy drinks.

Let us take a look at what caffeine does to your brain and body. If you are not sleep deprived, you do not have a need to drink caffeinated beverages first thing in the morning.

When our brain is getting tired throughout the day, or it has not gotten enough sleep, it produces a chemical called adenosine. Adenosine binds with adenosine receptors that are found in the brain, heart, and kidneys. These receptors are made specially for this chemical, like a lock made for a special key. It just so happens that caffeine can fit in this lock as well.

Adenosine is our brain's way of saying that it needs to sleep or get a nap in the afternoon. We will look into this in more detail in Chapter 13 about sleep. While our body sleeps, the heart rate goes down and the kidneys slow their production of urine, so we do not have to get up in the middle of the night to go to the bathroom. Or, at least, not as much as usual.

High levels of adenosine will make you fall asleep whether you want it or not. Because caffeine fits in these adenosine receptors, it blocks the adenosine. Because it also ends up in the receptors in the heart and kidneys, it raises our heart pressure and makes us pee more often. However, it does not get rid of the adenosine in our system.

So, if this repeats day after day, our brain creates new receptors and the amount of caffeine that was enough to block the sleepiness before is not enough now, and we need more for the same effect.

While caffeine remains in our body anywhere from six to ten hours, the effect it provides depends fully on genetics. Caffeine blocks these receptors only for two to four hours, effectively allowing us to function the way we want.

Caffeine is an addictive drug and the only drug that we feel comfortable giving to children. Because there is not enough information on the long effects on a developing brain, scientists agree that we should be cautious before we let our kids drink any caffeinated drinks or eat too much chocolate.

When people stop ingesting caffeine, they experience withdrawal symptoms that last about one week. And, after one week, the number of adenosine receptors decreases back to normal. The withdrawal symptoms include tiredness, irritability, sometimes anxiety, and a paradoxically hard time sleeping. I suggest that if you want to eliminate caffeine addiction, do so slowly and do not go cold turkey, as the brain can slowly eliminate the additional adenosine receptors and withdrawal will be easier.

The good news is that moderate caffeine drinking has not been linked to any kind of health issue. *Au contraire*, it seems that, in healthy people, it can have beneficial health properties. So, be smart about your caffeine consumption and for the best health of your brain, do not intake any within six to ten hours before bed. No need to beat yourself up if you enjoy your cup of coffee after lunch.

Alcohol is a popular legal drug that, in small moderation (especially in the form of beer or wine), can benefit your health by significantly lowering your risk of heart attack, cardiovascular issues, and provides good nutrients. However, it does no good for your brain. But alcohol can be fun, right?

Let's examine how.

Alcohol makes its way to all parts of the brain and dances with all the neurotransmitters I mentioned in the previous chapter. A human body can metabolize about one drink per hour, depending on body weight. Anything above that and the effects become apparent.

At first, it increases the activity of GABA receptors. GABA, if you remember, slows down parts of the brain. It does not make us think as well and sharp as we should. It induces the activity of glutamatergic neurons. Those are excitatory neurons that slow down parts of the brain. Like the prefrontal cortex which lets the person know that they are about to make bad decisions!

The release of endorphins and dopamine makes life so much more fun, and alcohol is happy to facilitate that. So, the person reaches for their next drink. After a few more drinks, it starts to impair the cerebellum, the oldest part of the brain, which is responsible for our voluntary movements and keeping us balanced. We all know what happens to a person's ability to walk in a straight line after a few drinks.

If this is happening on a regular basis, the cerebellum can become permanently damaged, and the person can have shaky hands and other motor movements issues even without any alcohol in the body. When the happy drunk person wakes up in the morning with a hangover, the toxic acetaldehyde that is left in the brain from the party is to blame. If having a hangover was not enough, this person may not remember getting drunk or even the whole event.

It does not mean that this person was a zombie and was not able to hold a conversation. Actually, to experience what is commonly referred to as "blackout", the person might not have looked drunk at all. So, why do they have little or no memory of the event?

It is because, at the time of the event, memories were filed in the short-term memory by the hippocampus. The prefrontal cortex was already under the heavy influence and could have been causing those bad decisions, like driving a car or getting into an argument that will not be remembered in the morning.

In order to be remembered, all the information from the event would have to be transferred during sleep into the long-term memory located in other parts of the brain, mostly in the cortex. For this transaction to happen successfully, GABA neurotransmitters would have to function properly to be the mailman. The depth of the blackouts is fairly dependent on genetics. So, while one person can suffer a blackout, their friend may remember the same night without too many problems, even if they were drinking the same shots together all night long.

While an occasional drink does not seem to pose any issues, drinking daily reduces the size of the brain and causes permanent issues. There is a common old belief that one drink per day does not have any long-term effect on the brain. To verify this, a study was conducted by the University of Oxford that started in 1985 and lasted 30 years. The results showed that, compared to non-drinkers, even moderate drinking was three times more likely to cause shrinkage of the hippocampus, the part of the brain associated with memory and reasoning. Those who drank four or more drinks per day suffered six times more likely the shrinkage of the brain.

Later, similar results were reached by Harvard Medical School, where a cardiovascular study was conducted in which subjects had also undergone an MRI at the end of the study. The conclusion? Up to you. Being a moderate drinker is good for your heart, but it does not seem to be good for the brain.

Nicotine helps with opening the pathway to dopamine. However, as with other drugs, the brain has the tendency to adjust, so what was good enough for the smoker at the beginning does not do it later on, so more and more cigarettes are needed for the same effect.

Nicotine can cause severe addiction, the withdrawal symptoms take longer, and can cause mental and physical reactions, like with any of the drugs mentioned above. Studies have shown that tobacco smokers cannot concentrate well without a cigarette. For example, when smokers could smoke during or before a test, they performed more poorly than those that were allowed to smoke during the test. So, if you are a smoker and planning to quit, do not do it during times when you rely on your high mental capacity. Connect it to vacation time.

THC, which stands for Tetrahydrocannabinol, is the most famous cannabinoid (out of over hundreds known today) in cannabis. Unlike the other cannabinoids in this plant, THC is psychoactive. And unlike any other drugs mentioned above, THC works more naturally with the body.

If you remember, we produce our own cannabinoids in our bodies. One of those cannabinoids happens to be anandamide. We talked about this neurotransmitter in

Chapter 10. It so happens that THC has the same structure as anandamide and fits like a key in the lock in the CB1 neuroreceptors that are all over the brain. Anandamide is our joy chemical, and THC does the same thing, except its effects are multiplied.

Most neurotransmitters work one way, sending a signal from one neuron to another using synapses. The ends of the synapses of a giving neuron are called axons, and the receiving end of the other friendly neuron are called dendrites. After the neuron fires, it charges the receiving neuron. It can excite or slow down the neuron. If the receiving neuron is excited, it passes on the information. This process is so incredibly fast that while you have read this information, billions of your neurons have already done this innumerable times.

However, the brain needs a break too. Under normal circumstances, axons and dendrites take a break after the excitement of passing on a neurotransmitter. The inhibitory neurotransmitters, that allow the break, come into play. The cannabinoid system that is already in place functions in the opposite direction and does not allow the inhibitory transmitters to slow down the neurons. This causes things like dopamine to be released over and over into the system. It allows the neurons to be excited longer.

THC is stronger than anandamide and multiplies this effect. Since it binds in the CB1 receptors, it is pretty much all over the brain. In areas where those neurotransmitters are present in large quantities, it affects the function of the particular brain region. For example, the hippocampus, which is responsible for the regulation of emotions, spatial coordination, and memory. All of which are affected heavily under the THC.

This can be beneficial, such as uplifting the mood. Although, in some cases, it can cause anxiety. It is not beneficial if you want to play sports, as spatial coordination is impaired. Memory is also temporarily impaired in adults. However, these memory problems can be permanent for someone using THC before the brain is fully developed, around the age of 25.

THC is, by far, the most fascinating drug in this chapter, simply because it works with a system that is made for cannabinoids. You will not find it in any other. Because this endocannabinoid system is our brain's cornerstone, the effects may be hugely beneficial, but, in some cases, not at all. While there is no danger of dying from an overdose, there are dangers to be considered.

I have been privileged enough to see research firsthand, and I have seen THC save the lives of cancer patients just as I have seen long-term users lose their minds. Although there are cases where long-term users have a psychotic breakdown, there is no evidence on whether these people were not primed before, and would come to that place eventually on their own, as cannabis is often the self-prescribed medication of people with mental health issues.

I will not discuss illegal drugs here, simply because I have too little knowledge of them and, I am assuming, that most people reading this book are not users.

At the end of the day, our lives are directed by addiction in some form. It does not have to be a substance, but food is technically a drug, as it alters the physiological state of being. Some people can handle addiction to things better than others. We all should be understanding of others and the struggles they may endure. Ask any barista how many angry faces she sees changing after people get their morning coffee.

Chapter 12

Memory

"One of the keys to happiness is a bad memory"

Rita Mae Brown

Memory is who we are to ourselves. Memories help us make sense of the world. Without having memories, how would you know what kind of person you are?

Every person in our lives is to us whatever our memory feeds us. This is regardless of any kind of objective truth, or regardless of how others feel about this person. The scary part about this is that it is pretty much certain that our memory is not recording our experiences like an independent camera, and is able to dismiss events, change details, or even make up stories. Still, imagine if you were not able to form any memories to begin with?

In this chapter, we are going to look at memories from a few angles. In one of my all-time favorite romantic comedies *50 First Dates,* you see what happens to a person who cannot retain any new memory. In this movie, Lucy, played by Drew Barrymore, has suffered a brain injury in an accident and cannot form any memories that last overnight. She remembers everything up to the accident but is unable to hold onto any new memory when she goes to sleep. Every day she wakes up thinking it is the day when she got into the accident. She meets Henry, who is delightfully played by Adam Sandler, and he falls in love with her. But because Lucy is unable to retain any new memory, Henry must make her fall in love with him every day. All they have for each other to remember is that one day and then her memory gets wiped off again.

The hippocampus is a tiny part of the brain that plays a crucial part in memory of all mammals. Damage to this seahorse-shaped organ can cause problems, like the ones that the Drew Barrymore character faced. While the hippocampus is not the only part of the brain that stores memories, it appears that it is the boss that sends out the messages with the instructions on how, where, or if to store the particular memory. I put the word "if" there because it is not scientifically clear if we store all that happens to us in a far corner of the brain and let the cerebral dust sit on it, or if we simply forget the events in order to save our sanity.

You may have heard about people who can remember everything that has happened to them since their childhood, on each day of their lives. This phenomenon exists but, contrary to popular belief, it does not make their owners happy. To be able to recall every detail of every stressful situation seems like a huge burden. Maybe our brain is saving us by forgetting stuff.

Why do we remember terrible things that happened to us in vivid detail? Why can we remember something so clearly after being exposed to the situation only once, while other times, like studying for a test, we have to repeat and repeat over and over to barely remember the gist of it? On top of that, how is it that, while we fully believe we remembered the situation correctly, it often adds or removes things?

When we recall a memory, we recall it because one of two things has happened. Either an exciting moment happened, or we repeated something so many times that the memory imprinted on us. The exciting thing does not have to be something positive; a negative memory may stay longer. This is for your own protection as a survival mechanism. The memory of being bitten by a venomous snake would likely make you more cautious the next time you are in a similar situation.

We need to remember the dangers that happened to us, or the chances are that we would have gone extinct long ago. Also, we are not the only species that can create this kind of memory. Scientists have tortured plenty of mice, rats, and other lab animals to prove what every person who ever had an emotionally scarred pet already knows.

Then there are horrific moments that we do not remember. This happens sometimes to the victims of long-term abuse. To cope with the abusive environment, the victim pushes those details out of the conscious memory. Nobody knows for sure if these moments are hidden somewhere in the brain, but many psychologists believe that they are.

I have talked to women that were repeatedly sexually abused, and some had suppressed the memories or details of the events. One said that she felt as if she had left her body and went to a different universe, so she would not remember the details of her abuse. This sounds like another kind of coping the human brain can implement.

A memory is always the easiest to create if it is accompanied by an array of senses and experiences. When your body is rushing with adrenalin and dopamine, you do have a better chance of remembering the situation. Although doing something will make you remember it much more than if you read about it. This is one of the reasons young children learn so fast. They remember things by doing them, not by learning about them sitting behind the desk in the classroom. Once they enter school and should learn using boring methods, they often lose their primal curiosity and desire to learn.

This is, of course, highly individual, but I think I can make a safe statement by saying that learning in the classroom setting takes a lot more effort than simply living it. I know this from learning languages. While in middle school, I did well learning foreign languages; when I entered high school, I was lucky to pass each class with a C.

Fast forward to the time after I left college. I became obsessed with traveling abroad, which was not an option for me when I was younger, and languages that I could barely remember then I have relearned within weeks and sometimes even days. But this only happened if I was in the country that spoke that language. Because I soon realized that anywhere I traveled, people would go out of their ways to help me if I tried to communicate in their language.

Side note, this was always my advice to people getting ready to go abroad. In every situation, try to say something in the native language of the country. Besides finding locals that truly appreciate the effort, speaking another language is arguably one of the best things you can do for your brain health, short- and long-term. Now back to the memory.

How does one develop a false memory? In the memory episode of the Emmy nominated TV series *Brain Games,* they created a false memory for a whole crowd of people. They made a short theater dialog scene where a lady had a discussion with a gentleman about fruit in the basket.

She never said the word "fruit." They named plenty types of fruit, like bananas, apples, and grapes, they even said the word "vegetable" in the dialog, but they had never said the word fruit. Yet of the people whose memories were tested, the most of them were certain they heard the word "fruit" on the stage. As the host, Jason Silva explained, "Our brain organizes all it is learning into the same areas, and the word 'fruit' is simply together with all types of fruit, so it is very easy to believe that one heard the word fruit which was never spoken."

Unfortunately, false memories can affect anyone at any point in their lives. In 1992, Peter Neufeld and Barry Scheck at Cardozo School of Law founded The Innocence Project. Per their own words, their mission "is to exonerate the wrongly convicted through DNA testing and reform the criminal justice system to prevent future injustice."

According to them, the rate of wrongful convictions in the USA is estimated to be somewhere between 2-10%. As low as it sounds, it represents anywhere from 46,000-230,000 people of the estimated 2-3 million incarcerated people in the USA. 71% of false incarcerations are due to false eyewitness testimony, according to the New England Innocence Project. You might be surprised how failing human memory is, and how easy it can create a false memory in the moment of stress. Suggestions from a well-meaning police officer can create a memory based on that. Suggestion.

Memories are shipped from the hippocampus to many

different areas. Some might not be stored in the brain at all.

What? Memory that is not stored in the brain? Well, the brain is still full of mysteries. The more we learn, the more mysterious it gets.

Implicit memory is remembered by our subconscious and the most well-known part of implicit memory is called procedural memory. This is that memory of riding a bicycle even after you have not sat on one for years. Some scientists believe that this memory is remembered by your body itself, and the brain draws that knowledge in the moment it needs it. In any case, it is interesting that people who suffer long- or short-term memory loss often remember tasks that fall under procedural memory.

The opposite of implicit memory is explicit memory. Both are part of long-term memory, but explicit memory is created by our conscious mind. There are two kinds of explicit memory. The episodic memory, where you store your own autobiography as you remember it; and the semantic memory, where you store facts you have learned ever since you were born. To identify an animal as a dog is an example of an early explicit toddler's memory, which can later be accompanied by identifying specific breeds and facts about them. But if you had a dog named Moxie, like I did, and remember petting him, that would fall into episodic memory.

I should not forget to mention the shortest kind of memory, which is sensory memory. This memory typically lasts less than one second, and it consists of the experiences you gather through your senses.

You are probably aware of the fact that memory, like muscles, can be trained. The more you train your memory, the better it gets, and this is true even if you are over 25, the age when your brain finishes developing. The best technique to remember something is to add your senses or muscle memory.

You might have heard of people memorizing long lists of names or numbers. Those people do not have an extraordinary memory. Rather they are using techniques and training to do that. For example, when it comes to numbers, they assign every single digit to a visual. And then they create a short story in their head, which is easier to recall than, let us say, a whole phone number.

I have created sets of cartoonish characters that I use to remember numbers. For example, for number two, I assigned swan because the shape of that number reminds me of a swan. Number eight represents a person with huge circular glasses, and, for fun, number three is a lady with a heavy chest.

If I were to remember the sequence of those numbers, I would create a story of a swan swimming in the lake, then a young boy with giant glasses comes to the edge to feed it, but the swan flies off over the boy, scaring him so that he runs to his large-chested mom.

In any case, it is great to practice. Yes, those solitaire and word puzzles help but, unless you are over 75 years old, you may want to add something to it. During young adulthood, these are simply not enough stimuli to save you in later years from Alzheimer's.

Before we wrap this subject up and move on to our next chapter about sleep, let us have a look at what we could do to improve memory.

Learning another language is huge for your overall brain health. The language center seems to affect all functions in our brains. Bilingual children do better at math and are more creative compared to kids who speak only one language. When a group of bilingual children was asked to draw an imaginary plant on another planet, the difference in results compared to the control group stunned the researchers. The bilingual children drew plants that had no earthy boundaries.

For instance, bilingual children were thinking out the box by making plants that floated in the air. On the other hand, kids who only spoke one language used funny colors and drew nicely, but all of the plants they drew were following general rules such as growing from the ground or flowering from the center. Somehow the ability to function in more than one language gave these kids the capability to think outside the box. How about learning or refining another language and taking a trip to the country you can use it in?

Learning to orient yourself in spaces can enlarge the size of your hippocampus. Studies have shown that London taxi drivers, who are known for having to pass incredibly hard knowledge tests of all streets in London, have a larger hippocampus than "regular" people. They did not start that way. Their larger hippocampus is a direct result of perfecting the spatial memory, which is well-established in all mammals and other animals. So, when you are on that trip speaking another language, use a map if you need it, but do not rely on your phone's GPS!

Get enough sleep. According to Princeton University, 40% of Americans get less than seven hours of sleep. Your memory is affected by this. Sleep is essential for storing information. I used to stay up late at night to study for exams — it was my own procrastination, I have no good excuse. I wish I could tell you that, despite sleeping for three hours, or in one case not at all, I aced the tests. But I did not. Despite the fact that my memory is quite above average (it comes with the synesthesia that I have), I was generally getting C's. And all I was tested on, I had forgotten within a week. The lack of sleep showed on my cognitive functions. In Chapter13, I talk all about sleep and how to help yourself to get on track if you are cutting yourself short.

Cut out sugar. Eating sugar causes problems for the entire body. It lights up the same receptors in your brain as cocaine, and it is more addictive. If you are severely addicted to sugar, try to measure your intake and gradually lower it. Replace it with fruit, which is also sweet, but the fiber it contains takes your body longer to digest. Be careful about juices that are stripped of the fiber, the fructose is in its simplest form and, even if the box says "no sugar added", it is full of sugar.

Exercise your body. It is probably no surprise to you that an active lifestyle is good for your brain and memory.

Meditate. Especially if you thought, *I would love to, but I have no time.* People who are in the need but do not act on it are setting themselves up for lots of stress, which will turn their brain to survival mode. It is useful when our lives are in danger and can even be healthy in small doses. But long-term, stress will affect your overall health more than bad food choices or a couch potato lifestyle. Meditation enhances the brain and those who meditate regularly, like Buddhist monks, display growth of the gray matter, which plays a huge role in memory.

Be mindful. This goes hand-in-hand with meditation but, unlike meditation, you can practice it in situations where you cannot likely meditate. So, the next time you are waiting somewhere, instead of pulling out your phone and letting your mind go into the virtual world, be present instead. With whatever comfort or discomfort there is. If you can be present to the situation well, you will not be bored, even in the most boring of situations (like in the waiting room at the doctor's office). Training mindfulness helps with focus and is a huge factor when it comes to memory.

Eat wholesome food. Of course, that makes sense. If you feed your body well, it can feed the brain well. One thing that may surprise you is that I am not going to recommend any supplements. Healthy overall diet? Absolutely. Recommending you consume a special herb that enhances your brain? I am not going to lie to you, there are not any good supporting studies. Actually, every single neuroscientist and neurosurgeon that I talked to on this subject agreed with an article published by Harvard Medical School titled "Don't Buy Into Brain Health Supplements." There are no studies that support any supplements and, additionally, there is no regulation. While there is evidence that omega-3 fatty acids in the diet, along with vitamin B, does help cognitive functions, there is no evidence that supplements contain what they claim. And if they make claims about herbs, well they are missing clinical trials and/or tests of the supplements. Not to mention the fact that anything for the brain must past the blood-brain barrier, a semipermeable border that doesn't allow anything that doesn't directly belong to the brain to get there. Although, placebos are strong and can do wonders for many people.

Chapter 13

Sleep

"Sleep is the best meditation."

Dalai Lama

What is sleep? Does it mean the time you go to bed at night? When your body relaxes its muscles and your mind drifts off into the land of dreams? Most of the time, that is the simplified version of sleep. But do you still sleep if you pop a sleeping pill and appear the same? If someone drinks themselves to the point of unconsciousness, are they actually getting restorative asleep?

Most people think that sleep is the moment when we are not fully aware of what is going on around us; that, in this state, our muscles, body, and brain are resting. While it is true to a point, as we still are breathing and our heart is pumping, this is not true about the brain.

When actually asleep, the brain is active. So active, it disengages muscles to keep the body in limbo, so it can go to work.

This ability to disengage muscles comes during toddler years, that's why babies and toddlers twist and turn in their sleep as they are acting out their dreams.

According to Matthew Walker, Ph.D., the author of *Why We Sleep*, we come to our conscious existence from a state of sleep that, in the mother's womb, the baby is sleeping most of the time. Healthy adults should not experience those involuntarily body movements as REM sleep supplies the body with a muscle paralyzing effect which we will discuss later.

Sleep is a reversible state of body and mind that is natural to every living being on this planet. It is impossible to live long term without any sleep.

According to a sleep specialist, Doctor William C. Shiel, about 80% of sleep is dreamless. That is what we know as NREM (non-rapid eye movement) sleep. The less common sleep, though more well-known, is REM sleep, named after the rapid eye movement that occurs during this phase of sleep. Nobody knows why that is, but scientists hold the hypothesis that it could be due to dreaming, as it is known that this is the dream stage of sleep. Both types of sleep are important for the brain. If there are keys to a healthy brain, sleep is the most sophisticated and important one.

While you sleep, your body is getting its much-deserved rest. Even if your organs are running to keep you alive, they are all running at a more restful pace. Not your brain, though. As soon as your brain gets a break from being in charge of all of you, it has to transfer the memories you made from short-term to the long-term, and then it needs to clean itself up.

Your brain cells, like other cells in your body, exist as any organism does. They need to eat, and they create waste. But unlike the other cells in your body that can use the lymphatic system to clean up, the brain has its own mechanism to do that. So, while you sleep, your brain is heavy at work. It never rests, which is quite remarkable if you ask me. During REM sleep, the brain is more active than while awake.

This brain cleanup is extremely important for your current health, as well as for your future mental and overall health. Brain cells eat more than any other cell in your body. The brain consumes about 20% of your daily energy, while it comprises only about 2% of the weight of your body. All this constant eating produces toxic waste. Those toxins are mostly cleaned up during the night.

Dr. Maiken Nedergaard, a professor of neurosurgery at the University of Rochester, referred to it as a "dishwasher." The cerebrospinal fluid is pumped between brain cells, flushing the toxins away. The cells seem to shrink in size slightly as if they tuck in for this process. Lack of sleep causes those toxins to stay and, unfortunately, they do not get cleaned up later. This is linked to many disorders including Alzheimer's disease.

No mental illness is accompanied by a full night of restful sleep. Whether it is depression, anxiety, or anything else, it is always accompanied by poor sleep. Now whether poor sleep is the root cause of the problem, or whether the problem is a consequence of poor sleep, is unknown to the scientific world. But if you or anyone you love suffers from debilitating mental issues, sleep may be the first thing to try and fix.

As I mentioned, the brain goes through two types of sleep. They do not occur at the same time, however. The majority of REM sleep happens after about six hours of sleep while NREM takes most of the time earlier. At that point REM sleep can last for about an hour while the first time it happens, after about 90 minutes of sleep, it lasts only about ten minutes.

NREM sleep goes through three cycles and ends with REM sleep. The cycles take somewhere between 90 to 120 minutes to complete. However, what other articles do not tell you is that those cycles are not the same throughout the night. Matthew Walker explains in the book I mentioned earlier, how lack of each sleep heavily affects the health of the person. If one does not get at least seven hours of sleep, they will not get the proper balance of sleep cycles, and the body will suffer.

During NREM sleep the body goes through the most restorative moments. Growth hormones are released in kids and the immune system is strengthened in all of us.

In the first phase of NREM sleep, called N1, you are falling asleep. It is that time of drowsiness and being half-awake. Your body can make a sudden twitch, which may or may not wake you. Perhaps you are married to someone like my husband, who falls asleep almost every time we watch a family movie with our daughter. When we wake him, he claims he was not asleep. He, like anyone else, does not easily recognize this sleep. When people are woken up from this sleep, they often claim they were not sleeping. This sleep lasts only about five to ten minutes and you spend the least amount of time in it.

The second phase is called N2, and adults spend the majority of time in this phase. It is still a lighter sleep, in which your breathing slows down even more and your body temperature and blood pressure begin dropping. The brain does not show a lot of activity, although it shows electric bursts.

The third and final stage of NREM sleep is the deepest sleep. This type of sleep is crucial to recovery and strengthening the immune system. It is hard to wake up a person from this sleep and, when you wake someone up in this stage of the sleep, they might be disoriented for a moment. You get more deep sleep during your early hours of sleep than later on.

After about ninety minutes of NREM sleep comes REM sleep that is known for eyes rapidly moving under our eyelids.

Newborn babies spend 80% in this stage, infants about half the time, while adults only about 20%, according to scientists and doctors. In this phase, the blood pressure rises slightly but the muscles are the most relaxed. According to Walker, this is so we do not act out our dreams. This function is turned on by the brain and it is developed during childhood. So, when an expecting mother is excited about her baby kicking in the belly and thinking her baby is awake, it is most likely asleep and acting out his dreams.

Most of the REM sleep happens in cycles closer to the morning, the second half of healthy sleep. Besides dreaming, in this phase, the memory is transferred from the short-term into the long-term. That is why it is important to get enough sleep during the night, especially for young people who go to school or college and need to remember what they have learned. So, studying throughout the night right before exams will not allow the brain to store the learned information.

When you were a teenager, did you want to stay up late? Or maybe you are the parent trying to get your teen to bed? My thirteen-year-old daughter complains that she cannot fall asleep until late. This is quite normal in teenagers.

While they need a lot of sleep, more so than adults, their developing brain shifts their circadian rhythm into late-night hours. Since I homeschool my daughter, I can allow her to follow her natural tendency and let her go to bed later and let her sleep until late morning. Although it sometimes means that her parents fall asleep before she does. My daughter is lucky in that aspect. I feel bad for all those middle and high schoolers who cannot fall asleep at night and then cannot wake up in the morning to catch their school bus. It is honestly not their fault.

After studying the brain extensively, I came to the conclusion that sleep is the most important factor when it comes to a healthy brain. Of course, it is not the only factor but, without sufficient sleep, nothing else works.

How much sleep do we need? Is there a way to cut corners?

Do you know that one person who claims he lives on four to six hours of sleep and functions quite well? According to Walker, there is, unfortunately, no way to cut corners. Those people who claim they only need a few hours of sleep are fooling themselves. If they do not see that they are cutting down on their potential today, they will pay the price later. Adults need somewhere between seven to nine hours of sleep, though we do not benefit from more.

Sleeping in on the weekends to catch up on a lack of sleep does not work. I wish I had better news, but sleep is not a credit card; you cannot spend now and pay later. For a night owl, such as myself, I wish I found a way to make it work. If you are a night owl too, you know how this world does not cater to people like us, but let me assure you that being a night owl is a true scientific fact and, despite what many life coaches may say, it is extremely hard for us to go to sleep early.

When humans still lived in tribes and had to worry about their safety, a small percentage of people got up extra early and a small percentage stayed up extra late. This resulted in only about two hours total when there was nobody on watch at night. This is in genetics and it is quite hard to change. Trust me, I tried and, I admit, still unsuccessfully keep trying about once a year.

What if one cannot sleep well? Are those sleeping pills or shots of alcohol helpful? Not really. The thing is, that even if your body looks like it is getting a proper night's sleep, your brain is not. Those pills, or alcohol for that matter, are sedatives. They sedate your brain and do not allow it to work. When it comes to sleep, there are no shortcuts. However, there are ways to drastically improve your sleep and increase your productivity and lifespan.

Here are actionable steps you can take to prepare your brain and body to fall asleep without any problems.

The first is artificial light. Especially LED lights or screen lights. Artificial light significantly blocks the creation of melatonin, the hormone which assists with falling asleep.

The next important thing that is as important is temperature. Nights do not only offer less light but a decrease in temperature. Our circadian rhythm also reacts to this, which is lower at night than in the day. Lowering your body's core temperature helps the body go to sleep. Obviously, you can achieve that by having a cooler room. I bet you have experienced hot nights where you could not cool off and you could not sleep. Interestingly enough, you can achieve a similar effect by taking a quick hot shower. Yes, hot or quite warm. Since it is a short shower, you would only warm your skin and not your core temperature. Your body then reacts by cooling itself from the core.

Then there is caffeine, which we talked about in Chapter 10. It takes about 4-6 hours on average for the body to process caffeine in a way that would allow one to go to sleep. This is quite individual, and, for certain people, this can take 12 hours while others can drink coffee all day long until the evening.

Alcohol, unfortunately, does not assist in getting a good night's sleep either. While it helps to doze off, it sedates the brain, changes its patterns, and causes what is called "fragmented sleep." Basically, if a person drinks a couple of glasses of wine to fall asleep, the sleep will end up being shallow with either the person fully waking up or simply not being able to spend time in the restorative deep sleep.

Lastly, it is important to keep a schedule. This is something I struggle with. If you keep an evening routine and adhere to the same bedtime, you are on a good way to the dreamland.

If you wish to improve your sleep naturally with my help, go to https://otakaraklettke.com/sleep and download the organized PDF with slots for you to check off in the thirty-day quality sleep challenge.

Before I end this chapter on sleep, I should mention naps. The "fun-sized" doses of sleep that people, myself included, love. It is beneficial to the human body and brain to nap, especially after eating. The blood is sent to the stomach to help process food. It is quite a chore for the heart to pump the blood vertically to the brain, so laying down horizontally, even if you do not fall asleep, helps your heart.

Short naps benefit your brain and provide the first and second parts of the NREM sleep.

By napping, you are significantly reducing the risk of a heart attack. Naps can also increase the mood, help memory, and people who nap regularly tend to live longer. There is a significant correlation to the amount of sleep a person gets and their lifespan. So if you have ever heard the party-goer's statement, "I don't need sleep now, I will get all the sleep I need when I am dead," know that such a person will likely get a chance to test that theory sooner than those who sleep the recommended amount.

Let me share a trick I use to get the most out of naps. If you drink coffee, that is. Have a cup of coffee right before your nap and nap for no longer than thirty minutes. My ideal time is twenty-ish but I know an entrepreneur who got his nap nailed to exactly sixteen minutes for his best benefit.

You have to drink the coffee quickly or ideally have a fast shot of espresso. The reason is that it will take about 20-30 minutes for the consumed caffeine to hit your brain. If you remember, the reason you fell asleep is because you had high levels of adenosine in your body. During the nap, the adenosine is washed away and the caffeine locks in the receptors. Therefore, you get up from the nap more refreshed than if you didn't have the coffee earlier. Just having a coffee without the nap isn't that effective either as the adenosine stays in the brain and is fighting to lock the receptors with caffeine.

Chapter 14

Sex

"The brain is the body's most important sex organ."

Author unknown

The reason sex feels good — or not — is because of the brain. Love and sex are the subjects, so let us explore how the brain makes it so fun.

I would like to address those that endured some form of suffering while having or being forced to have sex. If this chapter does not feel comfortable for whatever reason, feel free to jump ahead. I have the most respect for those in pain, however, I decided to explore only the consensual fun sex in this chapter. We will talk about normal chemistry during sex and what it can do for us. We will also look at the chemistry of "subspace", which is a state of the mind that a submissive partner can enter during so-called "non-vanilla sex play."

Obviously, the bartender in the brain hormone bar is busy mixing up all kinds of cocktails. Sex is one of the prime human instincts. The survival of humanity relies on sex, so it needs a strong drive and reward system in place. At first, the desire for sex is driven by lust. This is simply set by the release of estrogen and testosterone. Both hormones are found in both sexes, although estrogen is dominant in women and testosterone in men. Testosterone seems to increase the libido in almost anyone. This party starts in the hypothalamus.

Where there is a desire for sex, attraction usually follows. The hypothalamus is at work mixing dopamine and norepinephrine to stimulate our reward system. This is why the "in-love" period can feel so intoxicating and all-consuming. This cocktail makes us giddy and energetic, but it can also cause a lack of sleep and appetite. This is, according to Harvard University, due to a reduction of serotonin during the courtship. The lucky recipient can focus on that one special person all the time. In the case of teenagers, I believe that can override any focus on anything else in their life, including study.

Once sex finally happens, the front of the prefrontal cortex of your brain takes a vacation. No activity there. That is the part of the brain right above the eye sockets. This gives a whole new understanding of the saying "love is blind". Do not think that the rest of the brain is not active. Just the reasoning part. People tend to make poor judgments in that situation. In a way, it is a mechanism that also helps to prevent performance anxiety, so it has a positive side.

While the logical part of the brain is taking time off, other parts are super busy. The thalamus is active, keeping participants extra sensitive to touch, as well as creating or retrieving memories to help at the moment.

During sex and orgasm, high levels of oxytocin flood the hypothalamus. If you remember from Chapter 10, this is a bonding hormone that is released in women during birth and breastfeeding; however, during sex, it is released in both males and females. It is not the only drug released by the brain.

Among a whole ray of chemicals that are being produced, or getting ready to be produced during orgasm, endorphins play a big role. They suppress pain and can turn it into pleasure. I will get back to this in a moment when I discuss the infamous subspace.

Since pleasure is the reward humans (and I am assuming that animals too) get, it activates the same pleasure regions of the brain as almost anything humans derive pleasure from. Gambling, drinking, or even listening to music, lights up these same areas.

After the orgasm, the brain slows down and produces serotonin, which makes the participants happy, loving, and sleepy. Women also keep producing oxytocin, which makes them want to bond and cuddle after sex, while men simply want to sleep.

With all the flooding of hormones and our brain providing a "drug-like" high, does it mean more of those hormones could be more fun? Not necessarily. Excess amounts of dopamine can lead to jealousy, adultery, drug abuse, or even binging on food.

Similarly, excess amounts of oxytocin can, for example, make us love only those within our race, close circles, or religion. Any of the hormones are like double-edged swords. Too little of them and one participant may be thinking of her shopping list when she should not be thinking at all; too much of the same hormone, and she may feel raging jealousy.

Let me pose to you a hypothetical question. If drug addiction is considered a disease, should not the same be applied to people who suffer from hormone overdrive?

So far, we covered the hormones and the effects they have when we have the right amount and the danger of having too much. So, what is it about the subspace? What is it and how does it differ from what participants of "conventional" sex experience? Who gets there?

Subspace is a mental state that is the goal for the submissive partner during sexual activities that are generally referred to as BDSM. This state of mind is not possible to enter by the dominant partner, who is there to facilitate this for their "sub".

After interviewing people on the subject, it is still hard to explain what it feels like, as it feels different to every person. The common denominator is that it is a state of pure euphoria, loss of time, and often even space. The sub is fully present to her or his dominant partner. Often a burst of pain induces the release of hormones that makes the sub feel no pain and creates a morphine-like effect.

Participants of a Japanese sex art form of *shibari* often do not induce any pain but spend a long time tying their models with ropes with artistic precision. They use the term "rope-drunk" for their models during this ceremony. It does not necessarily involve any penetration. The high is clearly visible in the face of the submissive partner and once untied, the model seems unable to control any of her limbs for a short period of time. It is a completely altered state of consciousness.

Some refer to it as space where they are connected with the source energy of God, some feel a complete health and mental restoration. Many feel dizzy after as though they were drunk without alcohol. They all agreed it is better than sex. Like ultimate sports addicts, they seem to find themselves in the ultimate state of flow.

I tried to find more information about the brain being in the subspace. Getting into the subspace needs a life-fearing factor, which is always introduced as a form of play. A little pain is often, though not always included, and the threats are more visual than physical.

The brain responds with additional epinephrine much sooner than during so-called "vanilla sex". This hormone is the cause of the fight or flight response. There must be full trust established between the partners of sexual play involving BDSM, or the submissive partner can have a panic attack and hurt themselves. If this inspired you to experiment, please research BDSM safety, as it may be life-threatening or cause trauma when the dominant partner is uninformed and rules are not established ahead of the time.

To close this chapter, let us say that sex is healthy for us. It boosts our immune system, makes us happier, and more content in life. In the words of sex coach Alexa Martinez, *"If you can ask your partner to blindfold you, tie you up, and pour hot candle wax on you, imagine what you'll feel equipped to ask for at work."*

Chapter 15

Flow

"What is a normal state of the brain? Science doesn't have an answer for that"

Arne Dietrich

Winter Olympic Games 2018, Ester Ledecka is competing in two categories, alpine skiing, and snowboarding. The first is skiing. She flies down the hill. She does it for fun. No pressure. No worries about the audience. The truth about her is that she loves the sport, though her success in snowboarding is standing in the way of enjoying this sport.

So, there she goes on skies. Nobody is expecting anything from her. She finishes and finally looks around at the screaming audience. Reporters run to her, congratulating her on winning the gold. What? No, this cannot be the truth. She is shaking her head. They are joking, she thinks to herself. With her mouth open, she looks and feels bewildered. She won. She won! She won the gold medal in the super-G alpine skiing!

She is the world's gold medalist in snowboarding, which is her domain; skiing is just something else she is good at. Nobody in the history of her country, the Czech Republic, has ever won gold in that category. Nor had Ester planned on it. Her skies were even borrowed. Snowboarding was her domain and that was where she was expecting to bring a medal the way she had done in the past. This was just for fun. She did not place well in training. She is not a skier expected to place well. She came to get the medal in snowboarding.

There was no pressure to win. She did not go there to score this medal. She wanted to feel the mountain beneath her feet and the speed going down it. When her trainer was asked what the biggest problem she faced was, it was too much training. She was always begging to snowboard or ski one more time. That is what she wanted to do at the 2018 Winter Olympics — ski the mountain one more time without anyone expecting anything of her.

A week later she also won another gold medal in the parallel giant slalom in snowboarding, making her the first person in history to win two gold medals at the same Winter Olympics using two different types of equipment.

She experienced a state of flow. As Jason Silva, the host of *Brain Games* puts it, "Flow is the state of consciousness in which you feel your best and you perform your best. Everything is amazing and the performance level goes through the roof."

Flow is one type of altered state of consciousness that goes under the scientific term "Transient Hypofrontality." This term was coined by neuroscientist Arne Dietrich when the interest in the human brain was experiencing a renaissance. One of the perks of being an author is that, if you are lucky, you get to talk to great people about the great things the brain can do. In this case, I got an exclusive interview with Arne Dietrich for this book. In the world of people claiming their authority on the subject, I wanted to make sure I talked to the one person that was ahead of everyone else.

We live in a world where many people are claiming to be "biohackers". This term caught on like wildfire in a short period of time. No wonder since giant organizations like Google, or the United States Army, are seeking to find ways on improving the productivity of their people. Who would not want to perform at 500% of their normal capacity?

So, what happens when you get into the flow? Usually, time feels like it has slowed down, and so it is much easier for an athlete to, for example, ski faster. Because the prefrontal cortex is knocked out, you would take more risks. To hang on to the ski experience, you would choose to ski faster and risk things you would normally have to ponder in your head.

While risk-taking is one of the characteristics of flow, the failure rates of those risks are surprisingly low. Being in the state of flow doesn't mean you cannot get hurt. And, with the more flow states you experience, the higher the chances of injury are. However, if this is compared to doing the same activity and taking the same risks as you would under your normal state of mind, in flow you are making fewer mistakes.

Besides those attributes, your sense of self disappears. As if your ego took a nap with the prefrontal cortex.

The process which happens inside your brain when the prefrontal cortex is not in charge is like a party thrown by a rowdy teenager when the parents are gone for the weekend. Dopamine, norepinephrine, serotonin, anandamide, and endorphins are all released in the brain. New York Times bestselling author on the subject, Steven Kotler, claims that flow is the only time when all five of these neurotransmitters are released in the brain at once.

However, do not think you can get into the flow and become the world's best skier after one weekend in the snowy mountains. Flow utilizes all the knowledge you have acquired prior and takes away your ego, including the chattering, doubtful, pondering version of self. It takes the hard-learned knowledge and applies it with childish excitement. You are no longer in your own way.

First, you need to realize that to be able to drop into the flow, you need ideal conditions. Your brain needs to feel secure enough to let go of its critical thinking component, which it will not do unless it can afford to. For the most part, it is better if you are familiar with the environment you are in. This can be home for some people, for others, it might be a mountain surrounded by snow. You simply need to feel safe in your surroundings.

In the flow, you will do something you have done many times over. Since your brain is not there to guide you, it is left to your motor or other skills to do it for you. Believe it or not, you are still not reaching your full potential.

Your brain, while in flow, lets you do the activity within the limits of its capabilities. However, it also wants a challenging activity, so you will want to do whatever blows your hair back and do it at the level that is challenging to keep the excitement of the moment going on.

When I asked Arne Dietrich about the scientific hacks and shortcuts, I must admit I was hoping for a different answer. There is no magic pill you can take to drop into the flow. The science of today does not have that many answers on how to get in. We are lucky to know what happens in the brain.

However, we know techniques that can get people there. These are not new ones and can vary from person to person. While meditation is a good place to start for one person, it may be something different for another. Exercise is a common denominator to most people, but again, not to all. Being able to respect your individuality is a great place to start in your search for the perfect brain-tuning exercise. Still, we are all humans, so techniques from the whole pool of those we know can apply to you as well.

Try an exercise that will release helpful hormones in your brain and set you up for a day of being intentionally better, go to https://otakaraklettke.com/exercise. It is twelve minutes long, but the body posture, along with the recommendations in the video of what to do to enhance it, is my present to you because I want to see you do better.

It is also my form of saying "thank you" for buying this book. As the video is short and has exercises, it will work better and better if you can start your day with it consecutively. And, please, let me know how the exercise affected you by sending an email to smile@otakaraklettke.com.

Chapter 16

Brain's Blues

"Every man has his secret sorrows which the world knows not; and often times we call a man cold when he is only sad."

Henry Wadsworth Longfellow

A few days after my mom was hit by the car, when the doctors said that her condition was stable, at least from the initial impact, she lost the ability to form nouns.

I had one afternoon with my mom where she woke up after the accident and was lucid. I had a chance to explain to her what had happened. The powers far above my comprehension gave me a chance for one normal conversation. It is a moment I will be grateful for forever.

The next day my mom was moved from the ICU into a normal hospital room, and it was that day that my mom lost all nouns from her vocabulary. She would say something like, "Can you pass me that…that…that…" and pointed to a cup. The next day her verbs were lost too. It is hard to watch someone lose their brilliant mind, even if it is over the course of a few years. I watched my mom lose hers in only a few days.

I wanted to help, but I was helpless. At the time, my book *Hear Your Body Whisper* was at its peak on Amazon charts in the United States and Australia, and yet I could not help my mom's body. I felt like a victim of a cruel joke, as this incident happened after I decided to write a book about the brain. For some reason, I felt guilty about that. I was sure her brain would get better if we all looked for a solution, but the doctors could not tell me anything.

My mom had brain surgery over 50 years prior to this accident, making her the longest surviving person in the country after a brain surgery with a whole new brain injury. Because of this, no prediction was possible. My mother's brain was bleeding inside, the gray matter damaged, and her skull broken. I was losing my remaining parent. Her body made it for four months after the accident, but her brain could not recover. My mom, the person with two university degrees, lost all her brilliance in a moment when a driver did not see her crossing the road.

To write about this has been incredibly hard, but I wanted to share it because that event had changed the course of this book (it also delayed it by a couple of years). I dove into brain research on a much more medical level. I have learned that, while neuroplasticity is truly a thing, it is hugely overblown by many writers.

There are many occasions where the brain suffers, and solutions are not as simple as we wish. In this chapter, I would like to gently honor all those who suffer from problems with the brain. If you or someone you know suffers from a form of brain disorder and nothing seems to work, know that my heart goes out to you. Sometimes, all we can do is accept that and there is no shame in that. Nothing has seemed as cruel as losing one's potential. I am here if you want to tell me your story. Feel free to email to smile@otakaraklettke.com

The brain can malfunction for many reasons. There could be a traumatic injury, genetic predisposition, or illness that can fully alter the life of a human being and, therefore, the lives of those around them. Each situation requires an individual assessment, but there is almost always something that can be done to at least slow down the problem.

Of course, the best thing to prevent the cause in the first place is to protect your head from shaking your brain. Helmets save lives, but they do not protect the brain from hitting the skull. Things as simple as playing soccer and using your head to bump the ball can cause mini-concussions.

In 2008, in collaboration with Boston University, Boston Health Care System, and the Concussion Legacy Foundation, created a brain bank to better understand repetitive head trauma. After studying the brains of American football players, they found that 99% of brains from professional NFL players had Chronic Traumatic Encephalopathy, the kind of brain damage that alters their behavior and causes early dementia. Of players who played 15 years in their life, damage occurred in 177 of 202 cases. Sometimes, prevention can be picking up the right sport.

Obviously, people are born with different brains. Our society is quite neurodiverse. It would take a whole book of its own to talk about them. It can be difficult for someone whose brain is different, as it is difficult for the people around that person to adjust to the changes.

There is too much to cover, so I will not even try. However, I do encourage you to always try non-chemical help first. Meaning not pills. There are techniques like hypnosis or neurolinguistic programing, that can do wonders in some cases. Transcranial magnetic stimulation can be life-changing for clinical depression and it is completely pain free and noninvasive.

The problem with pills that are supposed to address the brain chemically is that often the brain becomes fully dependent on them. It wouldn't be such problem if they didn't have severe side effects. For example, to treat depression with pills may cause blockage of all natural neurotransmitters. Not just those causing the depression but also blocking serotonin and other happy molecules, turning the patient into a zombie of sorts. There are instances where medication is needed so careful evaluation should always be put in place.

I will, however, share a tip for those that want to help themselves or those around them. I cannot promise it is going to help, but there is a good chance it may and here is why.

When you were nothing but two halves that met, meaning you were a sperm connected to an egg and somehow the miracle of your life sparkled into existence, you were not anything but one cell. You enjoyed being a single cell, called a zygote, for about 30 hours before you divided into two cells. At the end of your third day, you were made of a whopping 16 cells called a blastocyst. You looked like a mulberry and were not an embryo yet.

To become an embryo, you had to start developing into something else other than the mulberry. You started developing your nervous system and the brain. This was roughly in the fifth week of gestation. There is a great video of the whole process published by the U.S. National Library of Medicine online.

As soon as scientists detect the presence of an embryo, they can detect the first systems that form the future baby.

The brain is formed by the endocannabinoid system that scientists in Israel detected in an embryo as soon as they detected the embryo itself. Side note, the endocannabinoid system in your mother played a critical role in nesting the blastocyst into the uterine wall.

It is easy to deduce that the endocannabinoid system deserves the same hype as stem cells. Stem cells produce the first endocannabinoids, which creates the nerves and brain. Many of the diversities in the brain that complicate a person's life, or the lives of those caring for such people, are the result of a malfunctioning endocannabinoid system. It can produce too much or too little of the endocannabinoids, or the receptors do not function on the level they should. With certain disorders, adding in cannabinoids, such as cannabidiol (CBD), can significantly improve the condition.

I ought to give a fair warning that while CBD is experiencing a boom, a lot of what is sold on the market is often not the quality that is promised to the customer. There is also not enough information for the consumer, and it can take a while to realize if the CBD is helping or if it is a poor brand.

My husband is a cannabis breeder and geneticist. His company works closely with universities to study his hemp strains. Hemp is a cannabis plant that has less than 0.3% of THC. Still, most of the hemp has extremely low levels of CBD as, in the past, hemp was bred primarily for fiber.

Before they worked on the scientific level, we donated a lot of medicine to people in need. There were two primary kinds of people that I have seen benefit from CBD and many others with different problems that did, but I would not call the data large enough to make this claim.

With kids affected by autism, we have experienced the most heartwarming testimonies. In every case of autism, CBD helped. In the hardest cases of children, I have experienced parents crying in gratitude and saying that CBD allowed them to see their child's soul for the first time. They experienced hugs from children that never initiated hugs before and the first, "I love you, mom."

Also, most people suffering from epilepsy did not get episodes while on CBD. This included a young three-year-old girl that, until that point, was suffering over one hundred seizures a day. The life of this girl was spent tied to a chair or bed at almost all times. After taking CBD, her seizures stopped.

Although those cases are amazing and by no means rare, finding good CBD is. If you expect me to pitch specific CBD products, I will not. As much as we wish to help everyone, we are not final CBD product producers. This year, 2020, there were many CBD product recalls, so know your source!

What I can recommend is to always look for full-spectrum CBD and not isolate. CBD needs the support of other cannabinoids to work its magic. Isolates work at about ten percent of the efficacy, from what I had a chance to learn, and, for the price of it, you would be wasting money and likely not seeing many results using isolates.

Endocannabinoids play the lead role in the life of a fetus and newborn. After birth, the mother feeds her endocannabinoids to the baby in her milk to continue the large dosage during the prenatal stage.

What about the brain's blues, that happen without injuries but through tough times in life? What about PTSD, anxiety, panic attacks, depression, and others? Are those cases of a malfunctioning brain? Yes. In true diagnostic fashion, those cases are problems of the brain as realistic as injuries or genetic disorders.

Often the changes can be seen using magnetic resonance imaging (MRI) or functioning magnetic resonance imaging (fMRI) or Single-photon emission computed tomography (SPECT) imaging. I would highly recommend that before you or your loved one agrees to any kinds of medication, you demand having the brain scanned. Far too often, psychiatrists tend to just guess and often they harm the patient by doing that. Trying cannabis either for CBD or THC if you live in the place that it is legal, is often helpful, however if the endocannabinoid system is overstimulated, it can have the exact opposite effect.

In cases like I mentioned above, for those that were triggered by life events hope for recovery is the strongest. Many people overcome depression or PTSD. The common factor here is the true desire and will to do the work for the person that suffers.

In brain injuries, the location of the injury in the brain is a key. If you remember the brain structure, those old part of the brain are the most affected in injuries and often fatal. While frontal cortex can often recover even if half has to be removed.

The hope for recovery is stronger the younger the injured person is. Age plays a huge role. Because I went through this with my mom, I want to offer my heart to those that are tired of hearing the gurus. Sometimes the situation cannot be helped. My mom had brain surgery as a young adult and recovered and got two Ph.D.'s after. Yet later in life, despite her children trying to do what we could, using every technique the modern age knows, her brain was not able to recover and in four months she lost her life.

Some injuries are too severe for recovery.

Despite it all, do not ever let your hopes die, as the brain is the most mysterious organ for those that study it. The neuroscientists and brain surgeons I talked to are in awe of what they have seen, but sometimes the brain does not respond.

I once traveled on a long transcontinental flight next to a brain surgeon. I am not sure if he was happy to sit next to me, but I took it as a sign to question him. When asked what surprised him most about the brain he answered,

"Everything about the brain surprises me. All other organs are quite simple mechanical objects that have a high level of prediction, but the brain is nothing like that."

I would like to end this chapter wishing you to keep challenging your brain, as well as keep it protected. Your brain holds within it your identity, quirks and talents and they could be lost forever in a flash of bad luck.

Chapter 17

Exercise

"You have to exercise, or at some point you'll just break down."

Barack Obama

The effects of exercise on the brain are massive. Yet, despite the commonality of this knowledge, not many people know why. In this chapter, we will look at the changes that happen in the brain when you exercise.

When it comes to the brain, it seems to matter what kind of

exercise you do. The most beneficial, according to studies done by many scientists including neuroscientist Wendy Suzuki who made a wonderful upbeat TED talk about it, is aerobic exercise. In other words, cardio. It helps to bring the heartbeat up, which causes more oxygen to go to the brain.

An oxygenated brain can make positive changes to itself that are immediate and long-lasting. Regular exercise literally changes the structure of the brain and protects it from long-term diseases.

Wendy Suzuki made a bold statement about the subject, "After several years of really focusing on this question, I've come to the following conclusion; that exercise is the most transformative thing that you can do for your brain today."

First off, you get immediate effects. Your neurotransmitters are at play right after your workout and your reward is a boost in dopamine, noradrenaline, and serotonin. According to her studies, it will finetune your focus for at least two hours following the exercise. Your reaction times will also improve, which can be a lifesaver if you are behind a steering wheel.

Then there are the long-term effects. These need consistency in your workout. For this to happen, you need a minimum of three workouts per week that are, at least, twenty minutes long.

For those not accustomed to a regular workout, this may be the point in this book where they will sigh and say that it is not something they can keep up with. I used to work out daily and, as I got older, I got lazier. But I found that dancing or taking a fast-paced walk with my dogs does wonders, and both activities are pleasant for me.

If I convinced anyone reading this book to give exercise a fresh start, access the free video I mentioned earlier where I combine the power of a fun exercise and suggestive self-hypnosis. This is a short video, but it is set to enhance your mental powers instantly. At the end of the presented video, you should feel an instant uplift of self-esteem and energy. Go to https://otakaraklettke.com/exercise.

Suzuki's research team found that consistency in exercise changes the brain. New cells are produced in the hippocampus, which aids the memory. They also found that long-term exercise improves attention and focus, which comes from improvement in the prefrontal cortex. But the most staggering discovery was the protective effects of exercise for the brain.

Growing the prefrontal cortex and hippocampus comes in handy during old age when those two areas are the most susceptible to neurodegenerative diseases. Let us say one was genetically predisposed to have dementia later in life. With exercise, the onset of dementia can come years later, or not at all. Basically, exercise is true brain insurance.

Other research from UCLA concluded that exercise increased growth factors in the brain, which makes the creation of new synaptic connections much easier. In other words, whatever you are trying to teach yourself, whatever reactions you do not want or want from yourself, whatever habits you want to implement long-term – exercising will make this much easier, because it will allow those synaptic connections to take place.

Exercise is also the cheapest antidepressant (because dogs cost money too). It suppresses stress hormones as well as aids in releasing all those feel-good hormones. When I used to work as a personal trainer, I had a client who started coming into the gym while she was battling binge eating. She never used to exercise but, when she started, she was not going to quit, and I could not have been more proud of her. One day, towards the end of our routine, she smiled and exclaimed, "I experienced something like a body-orgasm, just from doing sit-ups! How come this is not common knowledge?"

You probably heard of runner's high. That is the euphoric feeling runners get while running. But this is not unique to them. It can happen to anyone who sticks with the exercise routine. Back in the last millennium, I used to work out twice a day, at least three times a week, and at least once a day on the remaining days. Taking a day off was not something I desired to do, and I only did it when I traveled.

I know that there are many people reading this and thinking, "Well that is you, but I work all day. Then I take care of those around me and then I am too tired to move." If this applies to you in any similar fashion, try to make it fun. Take your dog on a speedy walk, go swimming if mobility is a problem, put on music while doing house chores and add fun moves to it (you should see me dancing around with a mop), and set a time for doing something physical for at least ten minutes every other day.

If you are not used to it, do not go push yourself and make large goals right away. Get there slowly but keep it steady. Set an alarm on your phone. Find a buddy to do it with you or even a friend you can text that it is time for you both to find aerobic exercise on YouTube. And, of course, get my video, which is free and is made specially to help your brain!

Chapter 18

Meditation

"Your goal is not to battle with the mind, but to witness the mind."

Swami Muktananda

Meditation gets a lot of attention and rightfully so. You probably would not be surprised when I say that people who practice meditation regularly live longer, happier, and healthier lives. They are not affected by stress as much as their non-meditating counterparts and can reset their emotions to point zero much faster, even at the times they do not meditate.

There are different kinds of meditation and, in various forms, meditation is practiced in all cultures all over the world. If you are a person who meditates, you are part of an estimated half-a-billion people worldwide who do this.

One of my favorite definitions of meditation is by the creator of Stress Reduction Clinic, Jon Kabat-Zinn who describes mindfulness meditation as complete, unbiased attention to the current moment. That is basically what Buddha did while he sat under the Bodhi tree and reached the state of Nirvana.

Meditation resets your mind to neutral. The benefits of meditation can be seen even in people who do not think they can meditate or consider themselves lousy meditators. But how? Meditation is beneficial but why is that? Let us take a look at what long-term changes take place in the brain while you meditate.

The brain is constantly creating electrical impulses that are fired between neurons, or neurons and glia cells. Those can be measured by an EEG machine, or electroencephalogram. You can think of those waves as music the brain is playing. At any given moment, the brain is playing a symphony. There is never only one instrument playing and some tones are stronger than others. There are five types of waves that shape the state of mind you are in.

Delta waves (0.5-3 Hz) are the slowest and loudest waves. Infants and young children are most likely to be in this state. As you age, you raise your frequency. Even in the deepest sleep, normal adults show few delta waves. It is kind of a pity as, during this frequency, the whole body heals on a cellular level. The cells rejuvenate. It is possible for those who master meditation and practice it for years to access this state of the brain.

Theta waves (3-8 Hz) are dominant in sleep and deep meditation. You can find yourself in this state when you are drifting off into sleep. These are also great restorative waves that bring peace into your life. If a brain shows too many theta waves at the wrong time of the day, it can cause depression or ADHD. When these waves are not present enough, your brain causes stress, anxiety, and poor emotional awareness.

Alpha waves (8-12 Hz) are in the middle of your states of mind. They create bridges between your subconscious and conscious mind. This can be accessed during certain kinds of meditation. Alpha waves are dominant while thinking and give you the power of being present to the experience of "now" and the feeling of relaxation. This state of mind is the most common goal of meditation.

Beta waves (12-38 Hz) are the most common during your productive times. Your brain experiences beta waves when you need to focus on completing a task at school or work. It is the state of mind I hope lasts while I am writing this book. Those are the desired waves during the productive day. Coffee and other similar stimulants help raise to this state when you are mentally tired. However, those waves settle down during meditation.

Gamma waves (38-60 or even over 100 Hz) are the fastest of all and are related to simultaneous information processing from different areas of the brain. People with learning disabilities show little of these waves, and they are rare. However, they are active during the feeling of universal love, altruism, and higher spiritual virtues. It is mind-blowing to me that these waves cannot be fired by neurons.

To the scientific world, it is not clear how these waves are produced. At the University of Wisconsin–Madison, researchers hooked up eight long-time Buddhist practitioners and ten college students who had trained in meditation for a short time as a control group to the EEG.

During meditation, the Buddhist monks produced gamma waves that were extremely high in amplitude and had long-range gamma synchrony. The monk's waves were in perfect lockstep! And they sustained it for a long period of time. There is no scientific explanation to this. I asked. The control group of meditating students produced a low amount of gamma waves and were not tuned like the monks.

During meditation, you are changing the waves. With practice, those waves become more tuned and have longer-lasting effects. Chemical changes happen in the brain during meditation as well. The most affected parts are the occipital lobe, which regulates attention, and frontal lobe, which is responsible for us knowing who we are and monitors the states of our mind. Basically, the part of the brain that keeps checking on you. Also, the amygdala, which is the part of the brain that is ready to freak us out and induce anxiety, calms down. The levels of the stress hormone, cortisone, subside.

Meditation can also be a reason for DNA changes. That is huge. If you imagine the DNA as a string, it is equipped with telomeres at the end. You can think of telomeres as the ending cap on the DNA, like the little plastic part at the end of the shoelace that makes sure the shoelace does not fray. As you can guess, when you age, those telomeres weaken. Like horse teeth show the age of the horse, what telomeres show are the biomarkers for cellular age. Meditators show increased length in telomeres compared to those that do not meditate. Scientists think this means people who meditate can live longer and look younger.

To summarize it all, meditation practices can help you focus better, stress less (among the things mentioned above, meditation weakens neuroconnections with negative triggers), improve your memory, boost your creativity, and make you a more compassionate human being.

I have met many great people who meditate and many who did not. Not all people seem to find love for meditation and even if they try, they get discouraged when it was not working for them, or they assumed that the point of meditation was to have a head empty of your thoughts. Buddhist monks call this your monkey mind. People do not lose their monkey mind. Monks spent years meditating six or more hours every single day to practice this.

Expecting to be able to not think, even from someone who meditates daily for a few minutes, is not realistic. So, if you happen to be someone who wants to start, but feels discouraged, know that it is a learning process that you are not likely to ever master. But you will benefit from it for sure, as long as you implement it into your daily life.

If you want to start, or tried and it did not work, start slowly with guided meditation. Go on YouTube and find a short guided meditation spoken in a voice pleasant to you. Or record your own meditation in your own voice. Meditate either first thing in the morning (that is what I do as "I am too lazy to get up", so meditating is a fantastic excuse to stay laying down for a little bit longer), or the last thing at night. Meditation can help you fall asleep and is a great alternative to other sleeping aids.

In my first book *Hear Your Body Whisper, How to Unlock Your Self-Healing Mechanism,* I gave away a written meditation for each person to record and personalize to fit their needs and heal their body. Although healing the body is not the focus of this book, I would like to offer this meditation to you as well. In the end, it will improve your brain too. Go to https://otakaraklettke.com/meditation to claim your copy.

Chapter 19

Goodbye

"Dubito, ergo cogito, ergo sum"
(I doubt, therefore I think, therefore I am)

René Descartes

We arrived at the end of this book. I thank you from the bottom of my heart for taking this journey with me.

Having read the entire book means your brain is focused and dedicated, which makes me happy. I want your brain to be at its best because, when it is, it will do more for you and this world in which we are all so connected.

I hope you have downloaded some of my gifts along the way and if not, do it now. They are all listed at the beginning of the book for your convenience.

If I could ask you for one favor, please leave a review for this book on Amazon. As insignificant as it may seem, every single review moves the algorithm. When there are reviews coming in, Amazon makes this book more discoverable. It gets a better virtual shelf. So, if you took value from this book, help others to find this book and write an honest opinion about it. If you have no time, even a single sentence will do. You can always adjust your review later. If you reside in the USA, you can leave your review here https://www.amazon.com/dp/B084VHK8CV

I trust you will take good care of your brain and, please, let me know personally how you are doing.

You can find more information about me, including my email, and my books, at www.otakaraklettke.com

Wishing you the best and I hope to meet you again – whether on pages of my other books, or in person. <3

Otakara

About the Author

Otakara Klettke is a former investigative TV reporter and current international best-selling author of Hear Your Body Whisper: How to Unlock Your Self-Healing Mechanism, as well as the children's fictional book series Detective Bella Unleashed. She is also a co-author of Holiday Hilarity: A Humorous History of Celebration.

Her #1 best-selling non-fiction book *Hear Your Body Whisper* became an instant hit since it was published in 2016 and its Russian translation rights has recently been picked up for all Russian-speaking countries.

The success of her book, her knack for communicating to a broad audience, and her ability to break down complicated subjects into compelling yet easy-to-understand information have earned Otakara dozens of interviews on podcasts such as Learn True Health, Discover Your Talent, as well as on other radio, webinars and workshops. She is available to share her expertise on health, writing, self-publishing, homeschooling, and the importance of reading for children.

Visit her at https://otakaraklettke.com/

ACKNOWLEDMENTS

There were many people who supported me on the journey of writing and publishing this book.

Thank you all from the bottom of my heart for helping me to write and continually improve this book. I cannot name you all but I hope you know who you are and that I appreciate you.

Special thanks to neuroscientists James Fallon and Arne Dietrich for their precious time to talk to me,

My editors Angad Bhandari and Maddison Tucker,

Proofreaders and beta readers that volunteered their time and energy,

And lastly my launch team that kept me going when I thought I was out of energy.

Made in the USA
Columbia, SC
12 April 2022